Life Retold

12 True Life Stories That Stir the Soul

Life Retold

Teri Hawkins

Voyager Press
Bend, Oregon

Published by Voyager Press
25175 Lava Lane
Bend, Oregon 97701

Cover Design: Gofinch Designs / gofinch.com
Photography: Istockphotos
Text Layout: Sheryl Mehary

Library of Congress Catalog Number 2008932748

ISBN 978-1-60643-472-7
Printed in the United States

Gratitude

FOR MY HUSBAND STEVE — MY ETERNAL BELOVED.

For Dianna, Sissy, Sandy, Joey, Tina, Jane, Mary, Jude and Tricia — my teachers of sisterhood.

For Christy, Kenny, JB, Benna, Jason, Adam and Cydnee — my "kids."

For my mother who nurtured the imagination of her children.

For my brothers who wrote my childhood with games, sports and laughter.

And for Kelly, who always has a story and who at four years old, only days before major heart surgery, pointed out an ostrich high up in a Ponderosa pine, explaining without hesitation that it was God.

The stories of our lives are not written in words -
they are told in glances and in touches -
in colors and in textures
woven from the mystery of our hearts
into the fabric of the Universe -
we spin our stories -
we tell the world a fiction made from shifting facts
that folds itself into our now
and whispers silken cords of words
that bind us to our sadness....

And yet the darkest night will flood with light —
the stormiest sea will smooth to calm
when you become the author of today —
when you let your yearning to be free
write the wordless harmony of now —
this place where all is possible —
where your love is
the effervescence of becoming —
where the Universe is your blank page
to fill with power
and with joy —
your glance
your touch
your mystery
your love
your story

~ Sam Smith

Contents

Introduction

WE ARE NOT MADE OF BONE AND SINEW BUT OF PARABLE and poetry. Life is just a story perpetually waiting to be told. Whether your life will be a drama, comedy, adventure, mystery, romance or tragedy is entirely up to you. You are not the sum total of your past experiences — you are the story you tell.

The way in which you respond to the seemingly clueless driver is your story. The way you react to the little habits of others is your story. Your future dreams, present doubts and past challenges are all just stories. Your life is your story — change your story and you change your life.

The good news is that you already know how to tell stories. You are a master storyteller, always have been, always will be. Everything you claim as fact, fiction, right, wrong, good or bad is backed by stories. When you justify or defend, you are telling a story. When you are grateful or forgiving, you are telling a story. You can stick to the same story you have always told and expect a different result or you can change the story, change the past, and create with a moment's thought — a happily ever after life.

We all love a good story. Stories entertain, awaken, challenge and sooth. And so it is through story that Life

Retold offers a journey into the consideration of your own life story. May it be an adventure of self kindness, acceptance, humor and ease.

~ Teri

Retelling Your Stories

AT THE END OF EACH RETOLD STORY YOU WILL FIND inspirations, ideas and challenges to assist you in retelling your stories. This is your time, so use it however you desire. Some may want to read all the stories and come back to the exercises; others may want to do the activities as they go. However you do it, it is your book to enjoy, your story to rewrite, so there can be no right or wrong way.

When you retell your stories use your memory, but use your imagination equally. Allow yourself to exaggerate when it works and to adjust anything at any time you are called to do it.

Life is a story to tell, not one to finish — so have fun retelling yours stories in as many renditions and slants as you choose. Along the way if there is anything you want to share with me, I want to hear it. Just write to me at www.liferetold.com and tell me your stories.

Monthly Contest — Retold Stories
go to www.liferetold.com
Prizes Vary

The Fright of
The Lullaby Voice

I'm a godmother. That's a great thing to be, a godmother. She calls me God for short. That's cute. I taught her that.

~ Ellen DeGeneres

AS A CHILD I ADORED MY GOD. HOWEVER I DID NOT blindly follow, obey, nor get down on my knees and beg to Her. I was more the stubborn, coercing, deal-making kind of follower. I would simply make my needs known and then wait for the Almighty to give in. I regularly tested God's ability to forgive and to punish. I did not follow God's commandments without question, nor did I worship my God on a particular day of the week. I found my God to be fun-loving, creative, athletic and hardworking. She had a wonderful singing voice and was quite proficient at spankings. My God was my mom — the one who gave me life, who created my world. It was to my mother I turned for safety, food, shelter, guidance, wisdom, nurturing, protection, attention and love. She was my concept of God and definitely, the higher power in my Universe. I was six when I first awakened to the Grace of my God. It came to me as I sat swaying dangerously high up in a fir tree.

I had done something that *She* didn't like. Only an hour before *Her* wrath began, I had been a gorgeous blond movie star, filming a dramatic scene from my soon to be released mystery flick. The scene was an everyday bathroom in a lower middle class home. I, the leading lady having just been stabbed by the murderer, was near death. Aware that I was mortally wounded, I was determined to identify my murderer before leaving this world. With sheer strength of will I pulled myself up to the sink, where I found a bright red lipstick. I was getting weak; my head was spinning from the loss of blood. I looked desperately for a surface I could write upon. The mirror was out of reach. I gave up hope and collapsed to the floor. Lying on the cool linoleum, my eyes were suddenly filled with a bright whiteness. I focused and realized I was staring at a brand new, cloth-covered, white clothes hamper recently purchased by the mother of the house. It was perfect. Bravely I crawled, lipstick in hand, to the object that would assure my place in history as a heroine. With the last vestiges of my strength I wrote clearly, "Mark did it ..." With great aplomb, succumbing to my injuries, I dragged the lipstick across the white surface as my arm fell weakly to the floor. My last thought was comforting: the serial killer would be caught. I had saved the world from further fear and pain. It was a good day to die. Then my brother, Mark, knocked on the door and said we were going to play hotbox, and off I went.

My mother was singularly unimpressed with my movie career. Actually she was livid. My dying scene meant nothing to her. The bright red lipstick on her new hamper meant everything. It was one of those days I was destined to incur the wrath of Mom. I was tried and convicted in a few brief moments. Defense was futile. My sentence was a spanking, inflicted by a switch that I myself was to cut. Personally I did not support this decision and so I protested like any creative, self-thinking, dramatic child of God would — who was closer to the door than Mom — I ran.

I headed for the tallest tree. Mom was in hot pursuit, yelling out commandments, none of which I felt compelled to obey. To me, safety lay in the big fir straight ahead. I reached my sanctuary and began to scamper up its trunk. Right behind me God was climbing in pursuit. It is a little known fact that God climbs trees. As an eyewitness, I will testify to the truth that God will do whatever necessary to catch an ornery child. Even at six I was aware that God wants to be in charge and does not warm easily to one of Her children ignoring Her word. I was equally aware that God could not climb or run as fast as I. My escape was not without a plan. I would continue to climb until I heard, *I give up, you win, come down and you won't get a spanking.* Those words never came, but I stuck to my plan.

I am not sure what club mothers belong to that teaches them to use a child's middle name to get her attention, but my mom was a charter member. A middle name does not belong to a child; it is a tool planted by the mother when she gives birth. My mom often used this tool with great results, but not this time. She played the middle-name card too soon in the game. My adrenaline from the escape trumped her. Obviously, she realized a need for a tactical change. From somewhere in the deep cellular memory of all mothers, my mother pulled up a tone of voice that froze me instantly. I don't know what she said, but her voice made it clear: *Stop immediately or you will die.* I stopped. The tree didn't.

I was an involuntary part of the tree's swaying. I had climbed so high that the trunk was thinner than Mom's patience. God's tone changed. She pulled out the bedtime lullaby voice. When in bed with sleepy eyes and warm blankets, every child loves the lullaby voice. When you are high up in a huge tree, it's terrifying! That lullaby voice was a sure sign that God was scared. If God was scared, what were my chances? I *was* going to die!

Being an uncommonly brave and healthy child, I stepped up to the plate and did what I had to do: I cried, I screamed, I yelled, I demanded, "Get me down!"

God displayed weakness, "I can't." What was this? My God was incapable of getting me out of a simple tree? Clearly my God was not omnipotent. Internally, I was indignant at her lack of Divinity — outwardly I wailed.

Things got worse — she began to climb down the tree. God was leaving me alone way up high in a huge evergreen. She was abandoning me. What kind of Mother would leave her only daughter in such a perilous place, alone? How was I going to get down? Was God always going to leave it to me to get myself out of situations that were not my fault? I mean, what kind of God chases Her beloved, sweet child into a dangerous situation and then leaves her there? Obviously mine!

As her feet hit the ground: "Can you see Uncle Jim's house from up there?"

Inward brat reaction: *What?!!?! I don't know!!!! Who cares???!! Apparently not you!!!!!* Outward pitiful response: "I'm too scared to turn and look."

The God of my youth was a persistent God. She did not give up on an idea simply because it was poorly received: "How about the bridge? Can you see the bridge?"

I was in charge here. Mom often told me she was the mother and I was the daughter and, by God, I would listen to her. I listened — I just didn't like what she said. I ignored her pathetic attempts at calming me down and screamed for the world to hear, "Mom, get me down!"

"Hey Sis, did you know none of your brothers have ever been up that high in a tree? You can see things from there none of us have seen."

Now this I heard. This was important information. Before fully committing to my reaction I needed confirmation, "What? None of the boys has ever been up this high?"

"Not even close. You are higher than they have ever been. So what do you see?"

I was higher up than any of my brothers ever had been. I could see things they never had. Getting down from this tree was really not that important after all. I was the world champion tree climber. My immortality was assured. No way would my brothers outdo me in this feat — they were bigger, and the tree would never hold them. All these thoughts happened in a split second.

God was prophetic. She used her powers to call upon an almighty motivator. Something so magical in its power, so profound in its influence; in all of history no one has witnessed a youngest child walking away from it. God had offered me a chance to beat my older siblings at something. I insisted she call the boys out to witness my feat. There would be no taking back my ability to rub this in their faces eternally.

When the boys arrived I emulated my oldest brother's all too familiar know-it-all voice, "There's a fishing boat in the bay. Looks like they're heading home."

Then casually added, "By the way, the tide is out."

Feigning boredom: "I can see the cross on St. Mary's, and Aunt Pat is having a barbeque — I think I'm going over there for dinner."

Brother Mike yelled up, "Wow, you can see everything — good job Sis." All my brothers were thrilled and kept yelling up questions. It was really cool when I saw the fire station doors open and the fire truck pull out and sound its alarm. I gave a play by play of where the truck was heading, right up until it pulled onto our street and stopped beneath the tree I occupied.

A ladder was raised toward me, and a fireman climbed up. The ladder wasn't tall enough. My fear returned. I was ready for the drama to be over — one can overdo drama, you know. He wanted me to climb down to him. I **froze.** No coaxing from him, brothers or mother could move me. I was afraid I might fall and he wouldn't catch me. No matter how professional, strong, young or cute he might be, the only one I trusted to get me down from my wavering perch was my skinny, weakened, fear-of-heights Mom.

Finally the fireman gave up, climbed down the ladder. When he returned he was not alone. I readily climbed into the stretched out arms of my God. The hug I received was the perfect punishment for *The Escape to the Mighty Fir.* However, for *The Case of the Lipsticked Hamper* I awaited my sentencing. Rather than imposing a punishment, my God left it to me how I should be disciplined. I willingly spent hours with bleach, hose and scrub brush to bring back the whiteness Mom had purchased. This form of retribution had a powerful effect on my future behavior.

I never again took a role where the leading lady had to wear lipstick. There were perks to that career decision. The women I played were of a deeper character, more independent than in previous years. My infamy was assured when I became the first female movie star who took off her heels, let go of the man's hand, and ran all-out when being chased by a homicidal maniac. From that day on, no murderer ever caught me. Sometimes I even outran my male co-star and we would have to re-shoot the scene. As for God, she never did become a big movie fan.

Retelling Your Stories

PARENTS — YOUR LIFE WAS IN THEIR HANDS, THEY were to provide your food and shelter, make good decisions for you and keep you safe. They had the power to punish and to bless. They were your first deities and you sought their approval and love. Here's the rub — your parents were human with all the potential in the world, however they were not Gods — at least not the kind who could read your mind, provide your every whim or know every answer to your unspoken needs.

Whatever stories we tell about our parents, become our truth. To retell your parental stories you need to first admit that your memories of Mom and Dad are not fact, but merely opinions formed through interpretations — your interpretations. Believing your opinion to be "right" is a societal story that does not serve us well in relation-ships and has created an epidemic of loneliness. It is part of the human experience that the "best" parents let their children down sometimes and the "worst" ones come through in amazing ways. Your parents are whatever your story claims them to be. *Change the story and you change not only the parents you had, but the person they raised.*

Every human has basic emotional needs. As a child we expect Mom and Dad to fulfill those needs. However, no person can fulfill the needs of another — not even Mom or Dad. Not only do we all differ in our level of emotional need, we differ in how we receive it, give it and interpret it.

Let's take a look at how you feel your basic needs were met by your childhood family. Please go with your first response as this is an emotional question not a logical one. Write down your answers and rate them from 0-5, with 0 being "not at all" and 5 being "completely."

The question is: To what extent were the following emotional needs met in my childhood?

Appreciation
Recognition
Safety
Understanding
Belonging
Love

Within the answers you've just given is a plethora of stories you've been telling to support your opinion. Start retelling stories with the focus on how your needs were met. For example, if you lacked a sense of understanding, start telling stories of how you were understood. Then tell stories of how well you understood your parents. You might also want to check out how your present emotional needs compare to those of your youth. You may discover simple but profound stories that have held you back.

Make mental notes of your discoveries. Perhaps you would like to use this as a journaling practice.

Cold Turkey!

The mind is its own place, and in itself, can make a Heaven of Hell, and a Hell of Heaven.

~ John Milton

EVER SINCE MY FIRST GLIMPSE OF HEAVEN, I'VE KNOWN it was the place I wanted to make my home. My first conscious visit to paradise happened the morning after a horrible binge. The previous evening my beliefs had been drugged with an alternative way of thinking. Yes, I was an addict — my drug of choice: Blame. It is a common belief that addicts will not change their ways until a significant event happens to wake them up. Well, this was the day of my significant event, and once I awoke to the paradise of acceptance, I never wanted to be in the hell of blame again.

The evening before I had decided it was time to confront my mother — I was fed up, and we needed to talk. She was done ruining my life. So, I called her to let her have it.

"Mom," I began, "we need to talk."

I was loaded for bear, ready for anything she might say or do. I was in control. I would not raise my voice, nor be overly emotional. I would just speak the truth for a change. I was determined to prevail in this conversation. Oddly, with all my planning for comebacks and posturing for power, I can't honestly remember what it was I wanted to achieve from this call. Anyway:

"Mom, we need to talk. I called to tell you I am finished letting you mess up my life. I have given you too much power for too long. Whatever success I achieve in life will be in spite of you, not because of you. You have done everything you can to push me down, stomp on my self-esteem, make me feel stupid and ugly. I am tired of wishing I had a mother who cared about me. I am tired of the tears of loneliness because my own mother doesn't even call or send a birthday card. I am finished with this family illusion that I am the bad egg and you the giving and sweet. I never again want to hear how difficult I was, what a problem I was, how impossible I was. I will never again turn to you for support, since you've never been there anyway."

I went on and on in a cutting, belittling, superior tone of voice. I was verbally violent, ruthless, and simultaneously exhausted by loneliness, pain and disappointment. I don't recall the words, but will never forget the cruelty of that phone call. I wanted her to admit how she had been wrong and had wronged me. I wanted her to take the blame for everything bad in my life. I guess I wanted her to hurt so much that I would hurt no more. I was living in Hell, and I was sure it was her fault. When the tirade of vindictiveness finally ran down I prepared my closing remarks. It was ugly and went against everything good left in me. I would not treat a moldy sandwich the way I treated my mother that day. I didn't yell; rather I spoke with a chilling tone that would slice open any mother's heart. It was dreadful:

"I cannot expect you to change your unhealthy behavior and so I am saying good-bye. You are no longer a part of my life. You will never hear from me again. I am better off without you."

Then, I paused.

It was a thick, muddy pause. I knew my mother well, and, as I said, was prepared. In an attempt at a loving voice, she would say,

I don't know where all this comes from. I have never said you were ugly or stupid. I have always said you are pretty. You did work harder than the boys to get grades, but I never said you were dumb. I have always been there for you, I just didn't do everything you wanted, when and how you wanted it.

Blah, blah, blah. She would defend her actions. This time I would not back down. I would not argue with her, nor allow her to think this was open for discussion. I had simply called to let her know the truth (remember I was in control — and yes, I'm being ironic). I'd planned this pause — it would give me the seconds needed to execute my grand finale. I would listen without comment to her tired excuses, and then I would simply say, *Goodbye.* And hang up.

Waiting for her response was, in actual time, quite short. In soul-time, that pause remains eternal.

With a voice as calm as a summer morning, thickened by contained tears, my mother said with true unveiled sincerity,

"I love you Sis, and I did the best I could."

I was prepared to ignore anything she might throw

at me, but she didn't throw anything. No pitching a defensive fit, no tossing a superior tone — she didn't even flip a sideways remark. She gave me nothing to catch, nothing to throw back. Instead she tenderly lay before me: *I love you Sis, and I did the best I could.*

I was stunned. I was speechless. I hung up.

Cold turkey! That's what it was — hard, direct, cold turkey withdrawal. It was a good spell before I shuddered into conscious thought. I was confused, and the foundation of my self-esteem was wobbly. I was in my own private twilight zone. Had I just talked to my mother? If I did, was she possessed by some other entity? If she's possessed, does anyone else know? If I had actually talked to her, if it was she who said, *I love you Sis, I did the best I could* — then where in the world did that leave me? More importantly, who did that make me? If she loved me and did the best she could as my mother, then how could I justify being the person I had become? It didn't fit. It didn't work. All my life stories of heroism, courage, and self-righteous justification would not work without a difficult, unloving, non-supportive mother as my antagonist.

My mind was moving so fast that my body forgot to move. I sat there, feeling my brain stretch. I was walking into the wilderness of my mind and getting lost. The new thoughts that were emerging were in direct opposition to my reality. I was arguing with myself — and I was losing.

I: *Just like her not to hear a word I said and to put it all back on me. If she did her best, I would sure hate to see her worst.*

Myself: *What if she did do her best? I remember my friends not being allowed over to the house because my mom was a single mother, and she wasn't even divorced yet. Her mother and father were so controlling, she never felt she could do anything right. My dad left her destitute with three kids.*

I: *Stop that! I've done that all my life: justifying Mom's behavior, feeling sorry for her, protecting her from anyone who might be tempted to say a bad word about her. This is about me. This is about how alone I am in this world because of her.*

Myself: *Maybe you have always defended her because you loved her so deeply and couldn't stand to see her hurt. Remember how you used to try to make her angry so she wouldn't cry?*

I: *But that isn't something a child should ever have to do. I was always afraid she would cry so hard that she couldn't stop. Then what would we do? All I needed was to know she loved me. I needed to know that she wasn't going anywhere.*

Myself: *She didn't go anywhere. She was always there — wasn't she? Maybe not how I wanted, but she never left. Imagine how hard it was for her to see her children hungry. Imagine how hard it was to work three jobs and raise three kids without any help. At 24, the age you are right now, she had three small children and a husband who was out with other women and gambling away every ounce of security they might have had.*

I: *I know all this. I've told it to myself for years. I still don't think it is justification for what she has done to me.*

Myself: *Ask yourself, really ask yourself: Do you think she loved you and did the best she could?*

I began to cry from some deep well of sorrow. I cried and cried, without words coming to my mind, without pictures of the past. I swam in boiling tears of pain. I went through moments of terror, believing I would drown. Memories of my childhood when I would yell in anger at myself to stop crying — fearing insanity if I didn't — began to creep into the present. For a couple of hours I experienced an alternate reality. I thought a few times that I might be a goner, that perhaps I would not return. With dehydrated tear ducts and a body beyond exhaustion it was finally over. I thought, "Breathe!" I took a huge breath as if I had been holding it too long. However, it wasn't that I hadn't been breathing — it was that the air had changed. My relationship with the world somehow was different. I felt cleansed, baptized in the fire of my mother's love. Admitting that my mom had always loved me and done the best she could was sobering.

When had I become addicted to blame? Being slapped in the face with, *I love you Sis, and I did the best I could,* had spun me abruptly around to see an entirely new view of life. I had no idea who I was in this new reality. If I had ever met myself here before, I could not remember. Throughout the evening, during the night and into the wee morning hours my thoughts were filled with endless questions and interesting answers. That night I began to rewrite the part my mother had played in my life, and as I did, my entire life story was changing.

By dawn I was pretty bored with my own dialogue and headed inland to see my grandmother. She loved to tell me stories about my mom. It didn't matter if they were all the same old stories, I would be hearing them with new ears.

Gramma: "Your mother was the sweetest child. She never argued, disobeyed or caused an ounce of trouble. She cherished her dollies and would cuddle them and call them her babies. Her dream was to grow up, become a wife and to have a little girl. Did you know that she wanted a little girl more than anything in the world? She picked out your name when she was just a small child herself. Then when you were born, she was so sick, we're lucky we didn't lose her."

I heard it — for the first time I got it. I had been loved before I was even a twinkle in my mother's eye. I had always been wanted, waited for. I was a dream come true for my mother. A dream come true! We were bonded by a dream from the very beginning.

Gramma: "Your mother never fought back or demanded her way — until you. She never let anyone tell you that you couldn't do something. I remember the only time your mother and your step dad, Paul, ever came close to a divorce. The fight had nothing to do with their love. It had to do with her love and devotion to you. Paul told your mom that 'No daughter of mine is going to play football.' It seemed a reasonable boundary to make for a girl of 13. Your mother was emphatic and immovable. 'If she can't play, than neither can the boys.' That was utterly ridiculous to Paul. He felt you needed to start behaving like a young lady. Your mom felt you could be both. The fights escalated over the weeks; she would not budge. I never heard how it was settled; I just know you kept playing football. To this day I believe she would have divorced the man she loved before allowing him to deny you an opportunity or experience just because you were a girl."

I had heard this before — from Gramma. What I hadn't heard was the devotion, the determination, the intention my mom had in mothering me.

It seemed all the tales Gramma was sharing said the same thing: my mother loved me, she had done the best she could — and her best was pretty good in a lot of ways. I was not born with the power of knowing I was equal to any man. I was not born with a resolve that no one could stop me from accomplishing whatever I wanted in this world. Those were gifts my mother had given to me, but she'd neglected to put a card with them to tell me they were from her. I just thought that was who I was naturally — imagine that. Mom certainly never believed these things for herself. What had it taken for her to give that to me? Creativity? Intelligence? Commitment? Strength? Determination? Heartache? Love? Who would I be had she not found a way?

Gramma: "I'll always remember the times I would find your mom in her bedroom sobbing because you were hurt, and she would not let herself coddle you. She would make sure you were okay, but she wouldn't baby you. She didn't want you to be dependent on her. She didn't want you to grow up being dependent on anyone. It was so hard for her. She wanted a little girl to cuddle, but that dream took second fiddle to being sure that you grew up independent and strong."

My mother had dreamed from childhood of a daughter. In that dream she didn't have to raise three children on her own, deal with a gambling, drinking, absentee husband, or live in poverty. My mother was purposeful in raising her daughter. She did not want me to end up as she had. She wanted to be sure I would always be okay. I'm thinking she loved me.

Twenty-four hours earlier my mother was uncaring, thoughtless, cruel and pretty much an idiot — overnight she became a genius. The same woman who had been the bane of my existence was now a light in my life. Where there had been sorrow — warmth soothed. Where there had been anger — gentleness rested. Where there had been blame — love played. Where once I had been the brave survivor of a horrible mother — I was now a blessed daughter of a courageous, wise, selfless, loving woman. This mother was new to me, and I was happy to meet her and the "Me" who she raised. I was looking forward to getting to know them both. Of course I had a bit of mending to do with my mom before we could move forward.

I left my grandmother's house and drove south to see my mom. When I arrived, there was no big discussion about what had been said on the phone. She did not shy away from me, nor did she passively-aggressively attempt guilt trips. I had torn her heart out, ground it into the floor and left it lying there. She simply picked it up and put it back where it belonged. Over the course of that weekend I told Mom that I loved her. There was also a time when I laid my head in my mother's lap and she stroked my hair, something I had never experienced. My mom finally got her dream, a daughter to love and cuddle. Who was I to take that away?

Please, let me introduce you to my mom: she is ga-ga about dogs, gifted with a crochet hook, and can remodel any house into a great home with only pennies in her pocket. Mom is grounded and practical. She is deeply shy with strangers, yet friendly; she's naturally kind, yet sincerely competitive; highly creative, yet funda-mentally conventional. She collects Fenton glassware and sews the most comfy flannel nightgowns. Mom can make a game out of anything and always finds the silver lining in the darkest of storms. Her wisdom is uncomplicated and grounded in her affection and respect for nature. She laughs loud and often just like her daughter. I used to be told I was just like her and would grimace in disagreement — now I smile with honor.

She doesn't enjoy meeting my friends very much because she thinks I give her too much credit, that I build her up too much. She would be mortified if I did not make clear that she is not a deity. She is completely and utterly human. She has co-dependent, self-sacrificing, passive-aggressive behaviors that I doubt will ever change. She has smoked most of my life and followed few of her dreams. There are things in the childhood of all her children she wishes she could undo, and she has a difficult time forgiving herself. She is not perfect according to the mythological dictionary that defines who we are supposed to be, but she is my mom, and I love her beyond perfection.

Actually I don't know why I feel like I need to introduce you to her at all. By now you probably recognize her, because you have one of your own. Although your mom may express herself in ways completely opposite from mine, she is one of the great loves of your life. Maybe you still have not noticed that her "flaws" are just a different hue from your own. Perhaps her love has been hidden behind substance abuse, mental issues, abandonment or even death. It matters not

— Mom is a love that you can write into the story of your life. So, let me assure you — no, let me guarantee you: your mom loved you, and she did the best she could. Blaming another person for their lack is an addiction that will keep you in Hell. Accepting love from that person is a choice that offers you a life in Heaven.

Retelling Your Stories

WE LIVE IN A WORLD THAT LOVES THE HERO. OUR definition of heroism carries with it expectations of unquestioning sacrifice and courage. When we become a parent we are thrust into the hero role. We are to sacrifice for our children and to have courage in all things. Where we are to obtain this sudden transformation is one of life's greatest mysteries. Additionally, we tend to ignore the fact that to have a hero there must be a villain and a victim. We often give our parents whatever part in our story that allows us to be the hero. To play this starring role we usually make Mom and/or Dad out to be the villains or persecutors. At times we make them into victims for us to rescue.

The co-dependency created through our obsession with the hero's tale is definitely one we want to alter. Below I have given you a few practices I have used over the years. They are designed to heighten your awareness, not to give you answers. Have fun with them.

I. Write down all the times you have thought someone did something that hurt you in any way. Consider parents of course, but also consider such relationships as a boss who was an egomaniac, the friend who borrowed money and never paid it back, the way your brother picked on you or the spouse who doesn't seem to care.

    a. With each one tell a *poor, poor, pitiful me* story. Dramatically exaggerate yourself as a pitiful victim until it becomes ridiculous. This is fun to do with friends, asking them to heap on the pity. Note when it goes from something serious to something silly. Are there degrees of victimhood with which you are okay?

    b. Now retell the story proving you were never a victim and how grateful you are for the other person(s). Explain how they were great teachers for you.

2. Take a look at politicians. Do you hold to the story that a leader's role is to solve our problems for us? How is this any different from the attitude that Mom or Dad should have solved things for you, done things for you, fixed things for you when you were a child?

a. Compare what you expect of leaders in your business and society with what you expected from Mom and/or Dad. Find the commonalities. Look at who you hold responsible or blame for what is "wrong".

b. Now tell a story of you being an active part of the solutions you desire.

Fox Trot Moments

People are lonely because they build walls instead of bridges.

~ Anonymous

WHEN I WAS LITTLE, MY DAD WAS THE BEST DAD IN THE world — well, in my world. He had the looks and charisma of Dean Martin, the heroism and strength of JFK, the gentleness and lovability of Jimmy Stewart. My dad was the best of every man I had ever known. Unfortunately, that was because I didn't know him at all. In fact I spent very little time with my actual father, which worked out pretty well, as my imagined one was just right. Real Dad-sightings were rare in my childhood — having been raised in a divorced home before divorces were popular. Actually, I was raised in a divorced home before my parents were even divorced. By the time I was born, my dad already had another woman in his life, and returned home seldom. I was nine years old before my parents legally untied the knot.

My childhood memories of Daymond, my dad, were few, but memorable. Some came through the repetitious words of my mother: "As an infant you would cry bloody murder if your father tried to pick you up." Or at moments of disappointment in me: "You are too much like your father." I have a visual memory of a time when he showed up, and for some reason my brothers and I had earned spankings. He didn't know the level of astuteness in his offspring, and he was attempting to convince us that the spanking would hurt him as much as us. At age six I was quite diverse in crying, bawling, wailing and howling. In my defense, I never sniveled — I was an all-

or-nothing kind of communicator. I had broken into my rendition of desperate uncontrollable sobs and was screaming at Dad not to hurt my brothers. It is worthwhile to understand that my father was notorious for his ability to schmooze, persuade and out-right con most people. I heard said many times in my life he could sell anyone the Brooklyn Bridge — twice. What he didn't seem to comprehend is that such traits can be inherited. While my oldest brother was into appearing brave, and my middle brother was a quiet gentle sort, I was a genetically empowered manipulator all on my own.

Daymond faced his "boys" and said, "I will drop my drawers and give you the belt, and you can see how hard it is to spank someone you love." Brother Number One denied the offer and raised his proud eyes to his father. Brother Number Two denied by bowing his head. I said, "I'll do it!" Daymond stopped for a moment. I remember his bending down and saying something to me, eye to eye. I cannot remember what he said. I do recall the feeling. It was somewhere in the neighborhood of "gotcha." I don't know what happened next, but I do remember my brothers did not get a spanking — nor did Dad.

Other memories were blurred between my imagined Dad and the real thing like when I was twelve, and my brothers and I flew down to northern California, where Dad lived. We piled into a Cadillac as big as my bedroom and drove to Disneyland. It was a long, hot trip — about a 45-hour drive if I remember right. Most of the trip Dad quizzed the boys on stats for every football, baseball and basketball player who ever put his little toe into the pro sports world. I tried to start license plate games and sing-along songs, which of course did not stand a chance against the ancient male bonding hormone of sports trivia. By the time we reached Santa Barbara I'd worked it all out in my mind. It was perfect. My brothers were lost boys we had found, and my "Jimmy Stewart father" was just making them feel welcome. After all, I was the one sitting in the front seat right beside him.

I was about eight when Daymond first moved to the town where we lived. He burst onto the scene dressing and acting just like Dino, a handsome life-of-the-party guy. We would go to his house for dinner and afterward he'd take the boys out to play some kind of sport. Not knowing that I was a ballplayer, my dad had me stay behind and help clean up the kitchen.

To add to the memories, I recall him being a big laugher, charismatic, adored by my aunts, uncles, gramma and grandpa. I remember he liked to win and usually did. He was very good looking and always dressed in the best of clothes. He was the one who introduced me to artichokes, velvet wallpaper and horse racing. He always had the best of everything, while my mother's beautiful skin developed wrinkles of stress just trying to keep us fed. I remember him trying to force my mother to have sex with him and my screaming, faking a bad dream to stop it. I remember him lying to my brothers and breaking their hearts when the truth surfaced. I remember he talked terribly about our mother, telling us she was a horrible wife, housekeeper and incapable of raising us. I remember him threatening to take us away from her. I remember I grew to hate him. He was the nemesis of my mother's existence and my mother was the center of mine.

Despite all this history, by the time I was in my late twenties, I had grown to genuinely love and admire my dad. Not the Jimmy Stewart, Dean Martin, JFK dad, but Daymond, my biological father. When I visited him, we would go out to dinner together, and then he would take me dancing at ritzy clubs. He only knew the foxtrot, but when he held me and we danced, I felt like a debutante dancing with an adoring father. He would tell me to stand tall because tall women were beautiful — short women were cute, but only tall women were beautiful. He loved to hear my stories about sales in my business. By this age I was able to see how intelligent, talented, clever, and in many ways generous my dad really was. I felt fortunate to be Daymond's daughter.

It is nice to imagine that he had a great wake up call and repented for all the devastation his thoughtless and selfish behavior had wreaked on my family, but alas, he remained the same person. He was not to be trusted in any financial interaction. He still lied more than he told the truth. He still insisted that every bad memory I had about him was wrong, and that he was the victim of my mother's manipulation. He accused my step-father, Paul, of being a bum whom he (Daymond) had to support. I defended Paul because I knew my real father had paid next to nothing in child support, and that my step-dad worked hard to give us a better life. Daymond's response was to throw red wine all over my new white dress. I left immediately.

Daymond had not changed. He was the same person, but I had forgiven him and in the process learned the empowering gift of acceptance. I no longer made him out to be any better or worse than he was. I would enjoy the good, strong, life-of-the-party, intelligent father and quickly walk away from those parts of him that were abusive. It was in loving my father that I learned some of the most profound textures of human love. In the home of our relationship, I learned love was not about the list of negatives or positives in another's personality; rather love was a choice — my choice. One cannot be a victim of love, nor can my love be denied by anyone but me. No one can withhold love from me, because it's an inside job. My father did not have a wake up call that I was ever aware of — however, I did. It happened when I was sixteen.

Sixteen is a big year in a young girl's life, and for my sixteenth birthday Mom and I were traveling one hour and a half to Eugene to buy school clothes. This had potential to be a great challenge, as we had drastically different taste. I was into the latest fashions, of course. Mom preferred the more subtle colors and styles of her youth. The height of shoes and length of skirts were bound to create a battle of some sort. But, the day was sunny and we were enjoying a mother-daughter phase of getting along fairly well. We climbed into our blue '65, three-on-the-tree, Ford pickup and headed north. In the midst of conversation I said something about my father. I don't know what I said, but it had enough vehemence, hatred and blame in it for my mom to react dramatically. She turned to me with tears in her throat, "Don't hate your father. If you hate your father then I have failed."

My mom had always been a hair-puller, not a face-slapper, but these words smacked me into a daze. She continued, "I never wanted any of you kids to hate your dad. If you hate him it will only hurt you. I don't hate your father — we both made mistakes, and what happened between us has nothing to do with you. If you hate him, then I have failed."

I tend to have a passion for logic. No one had yet labeled this as a primary source for my frustrations, but the illogical was deeply frustrating for me. My mom's reaction made no sense. I liked things to make sense. This man had done so many things to my mother that were cruel, deceptive, inexcusable and just plain wrong. If you matched me up against any of my friends, I could prove I had the worst father. He was a con, an obsessive gambler and had the morality of a wolverine — with apologies to the wolverine. Hate was a good thing to have for him. Why would I want anything to do with a man who had given my family nothing but heartbreak, poverty, abandonment and devastation? The only logic I could find in that was some sick desire for self-destruction — and that didn't work for me. I had not survived the fallout of his actions in my childhood to succumb to them in my teens. I spoke none of this, but then my mother didn't need words to hear me.

"Forgive him," she said, "if you don't, it will only hurt you."

Keeping my eyes on the road, I spoke, "Forgive him? Look what he has done to you, to all of us. Why would I want to forgive him? Give me one good reason, just one."

The tears had made it to her eyes. "Because he's your father, and I want you to know his love."

Much of my hate for my father had to do with what he had put my mother through. What she did on that fall day was take herself out of the picture. She did not want to be the cause of my pain or anger — certainly not of my hatred. However, it was not what she said that most moved me, it was what I heard from her heart. My mother had forgiven him. She didn't blame him. My hatred lost foundation. I had taken my mom's side for as long as I have memory. She had never said a bad word about my dad, I judged him by the pain, sorrow and stress I saw in her eyes.

I don't remember another thing about my sixteenth birthday. I don't know if I had a party, if friends from Portland came to see me. I don't have the faintest idea what clothes we picked out, if we argued, or if I even liked them. What I do remember was the gift of forgiveness wrapped in precious love handed to me unconditionally by my mother.

And so I can tell you with all sincerity, I am deeply blessed to have had Daymond as my father. I inherited from him an athleticism that would put me through college, a mind that made money easily, charisma that would cement a wonderful speaking career, daring that made life expansive, and an extended family that would forever support my life. He was the first person to make me feel beautiful and the greatest storyteller I've ever met. When my dad held me in his arms as we foxtrotted across a country club floor, he was Dean Martin; when he winked at me across a room, he was Jimmy Stewart; and when he spoke with respect about my mother, he was JFK. Okay, so he wasn't the dad I wanted him to be when I was growing up, but much of the best in me came from him, and I love him deeply.

At the funeral of my father, the son of his current

girlfriend spoke. Touchingly, he expressed how much Daymond had loved his sons, how much they meant to him. He had no idea my dad had a daughter. Every achievement, happening, moment of my life that would bring pride to a father had been, in his stories, given to my brothers. It upset members of my family that no one in his present life knew he had a daughter. It did not upset me, not even a little, because he and I both knew he had a daughter. He died knowing that his daughter loved him for exactly who he was. Not the image he gave the world, not the con he presented to everyone — his daughter loved all of him, just as he was, with total acceptance. Being a lot like him had at one time been an insult but now it is one of my greatest gifts. I got the best of my dad and for that I will be forever grateful to both my parents.

I had written my father every year on his birthday for many years. Each year I expressed my gratitude for him, my love for him, and the fact that I knew who he was. He would cry when he got those notes, and every one of them was sent back to me after he died. When my mother found out about his death, she shed tears. The love of her life was my step-father, but the father of her children was my dad. She had forgiven, and in doing so had given me a father and a life without blame, anger or hatred.

Retelling Your Stories

LIFE IS FOR GIVING NOT FOR GETTING. IF YOU LIVE 'forgiving' you will receive an abundance of blessings — beyond imagining. If you do not live 'forgiving' you will live for getting — forgetting your endless potential and who you were born to be.

Forgiveness is not a gut wrenching, difficult thing to do — that's just a story created and supported by society. Forgiveness is simply a choice that takes a fraction of a moment. You either forgive or you don't.

Nothing is unforgivable. NOTHING! Forgiveness does not say you agree with what you feel someone has done and it does not condone it. Forgiveness is not about anyone but you — it is totally an inside job.

Forgiveness is always available, always the wisest thing to do for your life story — no matter your judgment of the wrong doing, and regardless of who agrees with you. Forgiveness has nothing to do with anyone or anything but you and your stories.

1. Find the "Daymonds" in your life: loved ones who maybe have a different morality from yours; who were *supposed* to love you a certain way; who you loved but felt they did not love you. Then turn your story around by giving examples of how they did love you, gave to you, wanted the best for you. Create a story that proves how much they loved you. Find examples to support your claim. You can tell when the story really starts to change because you will sense an emotional release and possibly some revelations around your own power to love without conditions.

2. Consider someone who you feel has done wrong to you or someone you love.

   a. Let yourself rant on all the things that person should do to pay for his/her actions. Don't hold back, and forget being politically correct in this exercise.

3. Now retell the story, speaking only of the goodness and generosity of this person. Leave the word "but" out of the telling of your new tale. Make them the hero.

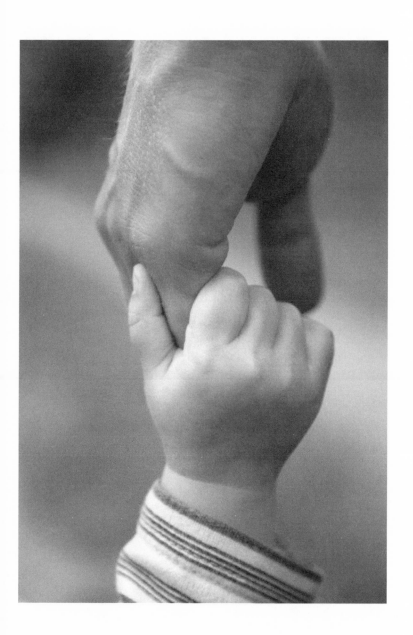

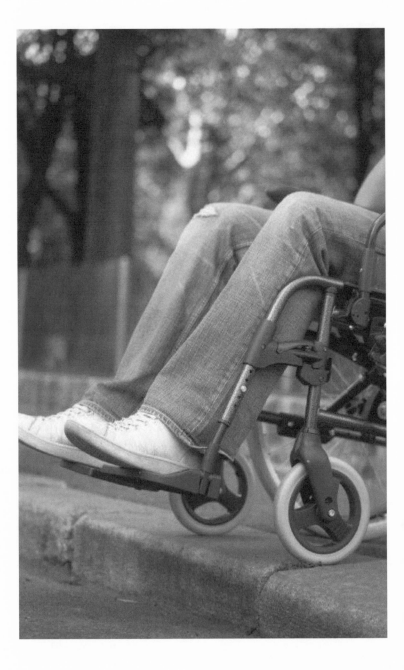

Pine Tree Courage

The vision that you glorify in your mind, the ideal that you enthrone in your heart — this you will build your life by, and this you will become.

~ Anonymous.

"BERTHA BUTT" WAS WHAT WE CALLED KIM'S HUGE tank of a car. She wasn't pretty but she got us where we wanted to go and offered seats large enough to camp in. Bertha, Kim and I were on our way home from an overnight excursion to the beach when suddenly Bertha left the road and began rolling down a steep embankment toward the raging Umpqua River.

When the spinning stopped I was awake, lying on my back, feet in the air, looking at the floorboard above me. Trying to get perspective, I turned to look out the side window. It had been replaced by the trunk of a huge pine tree. I wriggled around looking for Kim. My first sight of her was her blood-covered hands. "My head is bleeding," she said. I twisted until I found her face and was horrified by the mask of blood covering her normally peachy complexion. I found a towel and passed it through to her. She shook it out and pressed it against the wound.

Slowly we became aware of our situation. Bertha's engine was sputtering out and the river sounded like it was only a hiccup away. The drive shaft had pushed the floorboards up to within eight to twelve inches of the roof, dividing the interior lengthwise, with Kim on the opposite side from me. I righted myself to get a better perspective. Kim said her window was broken and she was going to crawl out. My exit was not as easy — I had to deal with the huge pine. I scooted downhill, toward the front seat to see if a door might open. In the process I got soaking wet. Bertha's front end was upside down in the river. I froze. Panic was certainly an option that passed through my mind. I chose instead to find a way out of there — immediately. As a child playing war with my brothers, I had learned how to crawl on my belly low enough to take cover behind the smallest of bushes. I'm guessing that is how I was able to wiggle between the drive shaft and the car roof to Bertha's other side and out Kim's window. I willingly admit that adrenaline at these times may well alter perception, but for me it seemed only seconds after I freed myself from the car that the mud gave way and all but Bertha's tires were submerged in the frothy water. It simply was not my day to die. That knowing would become important in the months to come.

Even though several younger trees had slowed our trip down the hill, that majestic, beautiful, courageous pine, which took a big hit in helping us, was the only tree around remotely big enough to stop Bertha's momentum. Even with the help of our friendly pine it was hard to figure out how the muddy bank held onto the car. Then there were the remains of Bertha's body after she was pulled from the river. Her engine was pushed up through the front seat, reconstructing the interior into a two-seater. Kim and I both felt like we had played leading roles in a tale of miracles.

After watching the spooky slow-motion plunge of

Bertha into the river, we began our ascent to the road to get help. I held my arm around Kim's shoulder and the towel to her head. She had her arm around my waist. When we reached the top of the hill we flagged down a trucker. He immediately called for an ambulance. A car with a parent-aged couple stopped and put us into the back seat of their car as we waited 45 minutes for the ambulance to come from Roseburg. All attempts were made to warm us up and keep us talking. Kim's face was cleaned up enough to assure us both that it had not been ripped off. She was sporting a pretty nasty gash on her forehead, but she was alert and her pupils were equal and responsive.

When the ambulance arrived the EMT put his head through the front window and peered back at us. I said, "I'm fine, take care of Kim — she has a head injury."

I am confident that if I possessed the skills of a portrait painter I could to this day, 28 years later, draw a perfect likeness of that paramedic when he looked at me. With wide eyes he said, "Don't move!"

Don't move? *Don't move!* is something someone says when a huge spider is about to crawl in your ear. *Don't move!* is something someone says if a mountain lion is sneaking up behind you. **Don't move!** are not comforting words. The moment he spoke, I was paralyzed. I mean literally, I was paralyzed. I became aware that my right arm was limp and had no feeling. My right leg was freezing, but my left leg had no sensation whatsoever. My neck had swollen so much that my three-button Izod was choking me.

They cut my shirt open: put a neck brace on me and an I.V. in my arm. They came in through the hatch-back of our hosts' car, put me on a back board and lifted me out. From the moment I heard, "Don't move," until I awoke in the hospital many hours later, I recall very little. The one memory that has echoed through my mind for decades happened as we pulled away from the scene. I was near sleep and I heard a soft male voice say with heart-breaking pity, "Looks like a broken neck. What a shame!" With that, my mind showed kindness and I left conscious existence.

I awoke to a new world. Before the accident I had been someone, an okay something in the world. I had been a star athlete. Basketball was paying for my tuition, track was helping with my living expenses, and life-guarding was making up the difference. My reality was as an athlete. There was nothing else I was good at, nothing else in which I measured up. I knew I was not intelligent, nor was I pretty. I didn't have the greatest personality, wasn't rich, a good dresser, nor did I have hidden talents in the arts. I was an athlete. This I knew. This was who I was, and it was my ticket to an education and an assurance that I would not end up like my mother — a single parent to three children and unqualified to hold a job that could actually feed them.

My ticket to a "better life" was my athletic ability. I had never been one of those teenage girls who had posters of male heart throbs, sexy models, or righteous bands hanging on my bedroom walls. I never pinned up cuddly animal pictures with "hang in there" witticisms on them. My walls had been plastered with professional basketball players, with Bill Walton covering the lion's share. Walton was a tall, red-headed, court-smart, passing high post. That is what I would be. That is what I had become. It was my ticket to survival. When I woke up, it was all gone.

Funny thing was, I didn't panic. The good news: my neck wasn't broken. Not so good: my neck had been inverted and twisted and the misplaced vertebrae had left me as a contra-lateral paraplegic. I was told this meant my right arm and left leg were both paralyzed. I was told I had a fair chance of regaining as much as 50 percent feeling in my left leg, and maybe as much as 20 percent in my arm. These numbers were presented in a hopeful tone of voice, explaining that with work I would be able to walk with a cane. I don't think it all sank in, because I can't remember being devastated by the news. Over the next four months I went to countless specialists in both Western and Eastern medicine. I saw several neurologists, regularly went to physical therapy, was adjusted by chiropractors and poked by acupuncturists. I tried internal medicine, strenuous vitamin programs and faith healers. All of this helped keep my mind busy enough to prevent over worry — but the use of my leg and arm did not improve. My diagnoses remained: I was a contra-lateral paraplegic.

At some point I became aware of my peril. My future appeared problematic. Would I still get my scholarships even though I could not play ball or run? If not, how would I finish college? What kind of job could an uneducated cripple get? I was sure I would not have to worry about feeding my hungry children, as I was confident my slim chances of attracting a man were now down to zero. Even with an alarmingly uncertain future, I spent a lot of time remembering the miracles that had kept me alive. My memories turned into a tale of gratitude to a car, some mud, trees and a particularly wonderful pine.

In thinking about that day, I imagined Bertha calling out for help as she herself was being totaled. I saw brave young trees, who had survived the tough first five years of tree existence, willingly sacrificing themselves trying to help save the lives of two girls. After watching the courage of his young students, the tall pine could not let their sacrifice be for naught. He stepped forward to stop Bertha from going into the water and becoming our coffin. I imagine his thinking, *If I do this thing I will take a severe blow. It easily may kill me; it is more likely it will weaken me so that I suffer a long agonizing decline and eventual death.* He makes his choice to help. I hear him addressing the muddy bank that had been his neighbor for many years, *Help me keep these girls out of that river, will ya Mud?* Mud jumps in with an *I'll do my best, Pine.* Well they did their best, good enough to save both of the girls from drowning.

Bertha did her part as well. With every ounce of her strength, no matter what happened to the rest of her, she would protect her girls. Bertha was completely totaled, smashed, leveled. She had only two areas where there was space for human bodies, the two spaces Kim and I occupied. I imagined Bertha, Mud and Pine hanging on to one another with all their might, waiting for me to get out of that car. I feel like they gave it every last bit of strength. Bertha's engine was already dead, she was drowning, and yet she held on until I was clear.

I love that story. It's a heroically sweet story. It kept me aware of the miracle of my life every morning I awoke. The color of life had changed for me. I was aware that my body was incapable of unassisted mobility. I was conscious of the apparent limits on my future. With all of that, there was something inside of me that had to be as brave as the mud, those little trees, that mighty pine and Bertha Butt.

Pete, my high school coach had once said to me, "Your body trusts your mind — it listens to it — that is a rare gift."

I had always liked that compliment. Remembering it had helped me through some high-pressure fourth quarter and overtime situations and I certainly was in a pressure situation now. There was no way I was going to sit on the bench and watch my clock run down without putting up a fight. I may have lost use of my arm and leg, but I still possessed the heart and mind of a champion. I grabbed hold of coach's words with the grip of a final second defensive rebound in double overtime.

I found a small, out of the way weight room on campus and began a lifting regime. I tied my right arm to the universal gym, and with my left arm did repetitions to exhaustion, then did the same with my legs. I would talk to my "resting" limbs, saying things like, *Enjoy your vacation. I'm just making sure that when you get back you are strong enough to play.*" I also would compliment my stronger limbs giving them credit for the lifting, not wanting them to forget how powerful and athletic they were.

One day the college volleyball coach, Jo, came in while I was lifting. I don't know how long she was standing at the door before I noticed her. She came over and sat down on a bench near me. Putting aside any small talk she said, "I would like you to play volleyball for me next year — are you interested?" Hadn't she heard? Still being in my more self-centered years of early adulthood, I thought everyone on campus knew of my difficulties.

Up to now in this story I have made myself out to

be quite brave, but it's important to note that I lived with such terror, that even looking at the next moment was too much for me. I was mad if anyone showed pity toward me and mad if they didn't. When ghost pains came to my arm or leg, I would cry like a baby until exhausted. I couldn't stand to look in the mirror because my body was all crooked and I couldn't fix it. My once even temper became explosive at times. I learned to whine, complain and feel sorry for myself.

On this particular day I chose a bratty, dramatic attitude from which to respond to this obviously slow-witted coach. I untied my right arm from the bench press bar. It fell limp to the side. Deservedly, I injured it. The coach said unaffected, "Looks like you cut yourself," and made no move to assist.

I, too, made no move; rather I said in my infamous smart-mouthed tone, "In case you haven't noticed, I can't even use my arm. How exactly do you expect me to play volleyball?"

She replied confidently, "Well, when you get it back I would like you to play for me." I told her not to count on it. Jo didn't leave. She sat there, not saying anything for a while. I grabbed my towel to stop the bleeding on my arm, then blatantly hobbled over to the leg extension and tied on my left leg. Out of the silence, without looking my way she said, "I got a call from a man named Wayne Peterson this week." Wayne Peterson was the most significantly positive influence in my life, as far as I was concerned. I admired him deeply; he had been the heart of my hope for years.

She went on in a nonchalant voice, "He told me you were a strong mental athlete and had captained his State Championship Basketball Team." I was close to tears at the mention of Pete, as all his players called him. I didn't even know he was aware of the accident. I couldn't imagine him seeing me in this condition. No way was I going to talk and have my voice give way to the tears in my throat.

Jo: "He thought you might be willing to try something with me."

I nodded.

Jo: "Lay your head back, close your eyes and relax."

All resistance gone, I closed my eyes. She took me on a journey through my mind and five years into my future. She asked me to imagine what I would be doing. I saw myself coaching a high school basketball team. During the visualization she had me describe in detail: games, practices, scores, plays and players. She had me tell her about my team's skills, weaknesses and attitudes. What made them a good team? What kept them from being even better? Who was the most difficult player and what was I doing about her? Eventually we ended up at State, in the final game for the championship. I was in the middle of describing a sloppy pass when Jo interrupted my account and asked, "Are you walking?"

My mind jarred. My thoughts stumbled: "What?"

She repeated, "You're at State, coaching your team. I want to know, are you walking?"

"Yes," I whispered.

"Are you using your arm?" The movie I had been watching in my mind was no longer just pure entertainment. I was being emotionally drawn into the plot. I was getting it. Eyes still closed I said, "Yes" with absolute confidence, "I have been waving it around throughout the game, used it to diagram plays, call time outs and give pats of encouragement to the players."

Jo spoke my name with confident authority and said, "Teri, what you see in your mind is the truth. Hold on to it. Do not let someone else claim to be more of an expert about your body than you. Your body trusts your mind — it will listen to it." In that moment I knew she was right. I knew I would regain the full use of my arm and leg. It was a done deal. All I had to do was wait.

While I waited, I learned a few things about myself. I discovered I was more than just an athlete. To my surprise I had a knack for improvisational theater, photography and life-drawing. I also made friends with a respected young local scholar named Pat. He looked a lot like Ichabod Crane — skinny, bony, with an overly prominent Adams apple — but he was a genius, and I had never had a friend like that. I found him fascinating to talk with, and he was an excellent volleyball player. This added bonus fit my plans perfectly.

Since the day of the visualization with Coach I had decided I wanted to play for her. I knew very little about the sport, so I asked Pat to teach me what he could. We laughed constantly at my ridiculous attempts at the game — and I can attest that volleyball is definitely a two-handed, two-legged sport. We persisted, and in the process became friends. One day, sitting across from him at the Student Center, he interrupted me and said, "You are the most intelligent woman I have ever met."

I laughed, loudly. "Look if you want to get me in bed, you could come up with a better line than that." I came to realize he was serious. He constantly commented on my intelligence, and I started to believe him. The day came when I thought I might be smart enough to read a book cover to cover. I had never done that. In school, when asked to do book reports, I had always read the first and last chapters and written the report from there. I thought I was too dumb to read an entire book. My mind had always known I was good for only one thing. My mind was changing.

Six months after that visualization with Coach Jo in the weight room, I was awakened by a hand on my face. I quickly grabbed it and threw it off of me, simultaneously rising to defend myself. The offending limb made a horrible thud against the sideboard of the bed, and I cried out in pain. My right arm was throbbing. I had feeling in my right arm! Never before or since have I been as happy about pain. I instantly sprang out of bed to race and tell my roommates and fell flat on my face. My leg had not yet awakened from its many months of slumber. The noise brought the troops racing in to save the day - instead we all ended up on the floor in belly laughs that had been waiting to explode for almost a year.

X-rays were taken and they proved it — I was still paralyzed. There was no medical reason for me to have the use of my arm. The doctor said it was likely just a temporary thing. He may well have been right -but he was wrong. Not only have I had the use of my strong, powerful, athletic arm for over 30 years, it was only weeks after his diagnosis that my leg returned as well — a bit more than *temporary* recovery.

Once sensation had returned to my arm I could hardly wait to get my strength back. The doctors told me to wait. Wait for what? To see if they were right? To make sure it was temporary? Because if I lifted weights I might lose the use of my limbs?

What you see in your mind is the truth. Hold on to it. Do not let someone else claim to be more of an expert about your body than you. Your body trusts your mind — it will listen to it. I saw a future where I was walking and using my arm. I went home, picked up a can of black beans and began my strength training. Ten reps with the can and my arm gave up. By the time my leg regained feeling I was up to thirty reps with the can. The leg took a bit longer. The first day I barely made it up two stairs, and it was almost a month before I made it unassisted to the second floor of the apartment. Within six months I was playing volleyball for Jo.

Over the years I have had days, even weeks, when my arm or leg will go to sleep for a while. I bless it, wish it well and wait for its return. It always comes home, and I always welcome it back with love and admiration.

I was paralyzed long before that accident. My fears, doubts and beliefs had crippled me. I thought I was a product of my upbringing, my environment, my disappointments, genes and other people. The accident made me aware that I had choices. Nothing in life is against me, or even a problem, without my thinking it so. It was this event that started me on the path to accepting myself, forgiving my parents and fulfilling my dreams. This was the incident that made me aware that my life is what I make it. This miracle cemented in me the knowing that reality is what I think it is, and no one, no matter their expertise, experience or knowledge, knows my reality but **me.**

My life is not what is given to me as an experience — it is how I choose to interpret that experience. Today, there is no doubt I have a miraculous life filled with wonders beyond imagination. Am I one of the lucky ones? Sure am! Do I live a blessed life? Sure do! Why me? What makes me so special? Why am I so fortunate? That's easy: I think I am.

Retelling Your Story

I BELIEVE WE EACH HAVE A LIMITLESS SUPPLY OF INNER courage that when discovered reduces our need to be heroes in the outer world. Being a hero is a great thing when an unexpected trauma or danger occurs; the problem comes when we start creating the dangers and traumas so that we have a place to prove our heroism — to Self and to others. When we discover our inner courage however, the need for outer recognition diminishes and eventually disappears. So what is the secret? How do we uncover this healing resource? Do we have to recover from paralysis to find it? Please don't! Only the most remedial of humans need the kind of trauma I created for myself. In 30 years of speaking and teaching around the miracle of my recovery, I have created many experiences for the discovery of inner courage without the horrors or melodramas.

Below is a client favorite. Do this for fun, not as another chore.

I.   Write a list of your dreams. Things you have always wanted to do. Big things, little things, expensive, cheap, long, short, easy and "impossible." Write them down. Once you feel complete with the list go to Number Two.

2. For each thing on your list write the reason you have not done it yet.

3. Identify your top three most repeated reasons (excuses). For example: I don't have the money, not enough time, I am too old, it's too late.

4. Laughter is a powerful key to unlocking your inner courage so we are going to create three ridiculous excuses to replace your old tired delusional ones. Example: You're late for a board meeting. Rather than say, "The traffic...." I would say: "I couldn't find the axe" or "The sky was the wrong shade of blue yesterday." If you have kids, use their genius in this. You can even have a party to find juicy, outrageous, laughable excuses.

5. Now use only your bizarre excuses for where you would normally use your old stand by ones. You can spread this exercise to the people in your life. What happens is exciting, amazing and often life changing. Most importantly, it sets free a courage that has waited a lifetime to come into the light of your world.

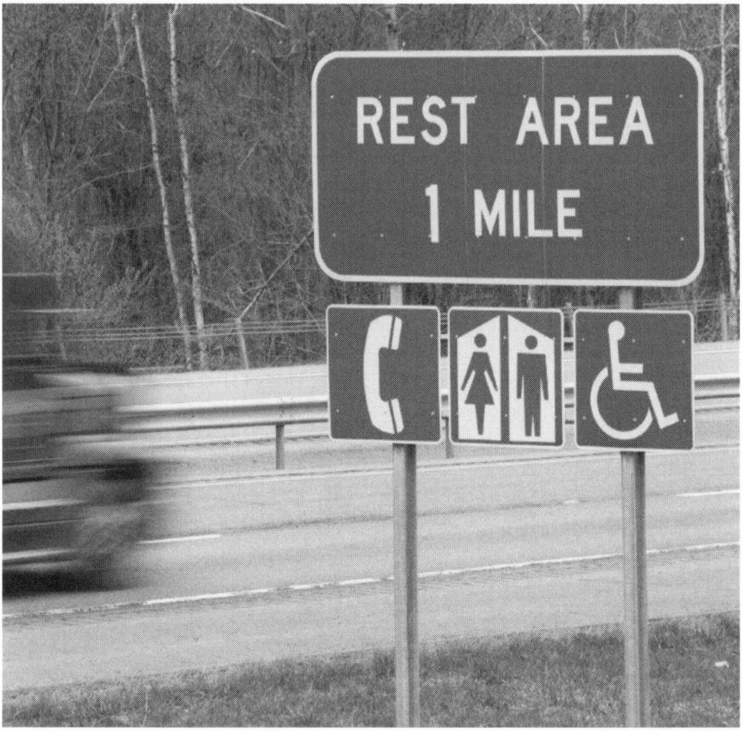
REST AREA
1 MILE

A Brain Rebooted

'Tain't no greater ignoramus in this world than someone who turns his nose up at something he don't know nothin' about.

~ Grandpa, a very wise uneducated man.

WE WERE ON CHRISTMAS BREAK, MY FRIEND DIANE and I. We had decided to head for the Bay area. My father lived in Napa, the heart of California's wine country, so that would be our home base. We also thought we might pick up some extra cash by playing in a doubles grass volleyball tournament in Santa Barbara. My brother, Mark, was going to be in town at the same time so we would hook up with him and pal around. Exhausted from a finals week of cramming and exhilarated that it was all over, we headed out in my Datsun pickup. Snow and ice on the pass turned a six-hour drive into nine. I could not have had a better partner for the trip. We played games, sang songs, talked about guys. Diane supported me completely, keeping me alert and awake. My father warmly greeted us when we arrived at two o'clock on Friday morning.

Diane was an easy friend to have. She was uncomplicated, entertaining and pretty much game for anything. Neither of us had gone through the stage where laughing was un-cool and we could lose it in a giggle-fest as completely as any adolescent. Our friendship was a team. We had each other's back and we never doubted it. This natural movement with one another originated on the volleyball court. Diane had springs, was agile and explosive physically. She played with abandon and joy, filled with amazing raw physical talent. She had moments of genius at the net, but her magic, her power, was in the back row. When Di was in the back row we all knew the ball was coming up. It wasn't just that she could fly through the air with the greatest of ease and dig an impossible shot, it was the way she led the entire team defensively when she was back there. She would call a shot before it was hit, positioning us with her words. I marveled many times at her ability to be deep in center-back when an opposing hitter would go up, cock her arm to hit the ball, and suddenly change up, tipping it barely over the block — right into Di's waiting hands. How she'd get there without freezing time was a great mystery. It was also a key to our amazing season. For me Diane was the lightness of the team. When we were in the back row together, I excelled. I trusted, respected, admired, appreciated and really liked Di. She was a friend. I loved her.

Our Christmas break excursion was great. We had very little sleep and a whole lot of fun. We did the crazy, the silly and the stupid — like all college students are destined to do. We averaged no more than three hours of sleep a night and came home with $75 each, left over from our volleyball winnings. We began our trip home five days before classes were to resume because I was going to move in and share a house with Di and Mary. Somewhere in about the sixth hour of driving, Diane went quiet, staring out the side window. I listened to music until she reached over, turned it down and said,

"I have something I have to tell you."

She looked back out her window; whatever it was she had to say, Diane was uncomfortable. I had been expecting something like this. The house they lived in was a nice place. Mary knew the owners and they had trusted her with what had been their home for many years. Unfortunately, their most recent roommate had done some damage to the place and financially left Mary and Di with the repairs. I thought maybe they would want me to sign some agreement so this would not happen again. I was fine with that and I wanted to ease Diane's angst, so I told her right away, "Look, Di, whatever you and Mary need me to sign to make you feel comfortable, I'll sign. I trust you both; don't feel badly for asking me."

Di said nothing. She just stared out her window. Something was wrong. Maybe they had changed their mind about me moving in at all. Maybe they wanted to ask me for more rent and knew that I couldn't afford more. Whatever was going on, this was not Diane-typical behavior. I asked, "What is it? Tell me."

Without turning to look at me she said,

"I love Mary."

I was tracking. I assured her, "I know you do. I love her too, and you."

"No," she said with resignation, "I **love** Mary."

What was going on? Why was this so important to get me to understand before she told me what was wrong?

Was there something wrong with Mary? Was she sick? What was the "but" that Di had not yet told me. She loved Mary, but...? But what?

Diane turned to look at me. "You don't understand. Mary and I are in love."

I still remember exactly where we were on I-5 when what Diane said finally met my ears, hugged my brain, and ignited my understanding. I remember where my hands were placed on the steering wheel. I remember the streaks of trees shadowing the road. I even remember rounding a corner and seeing a "Rest Area one-mile" sign. In my world I had no reference for this conversation. My brain was like a hard drive getting a download, and I was waiting for it to finish before I could function again.

I was raised to believe that homosexuality is a mental illness. My mother and stepfather are what we in America call "good people." They pay their taxes, work for a living to keep food on the table and a roof over their family's head. My parents did not present their morality or judgments to their children as possibilities — they fed them as facts. What I knew of the world was that *homosexuality is a sickness.* I had always been clear that I wanted nothing to do with fags or freaks. I never questioned that same-sex partnerships were depraved and psychologically sick. It was all too seedy for my All-American illusion.

My processor worked fairly fast and the download took very little time. It was clear we had to talk. She was my friend and I had to be honest. I had to tell her how I felt and we would work it out. I spoke up, "You and Mary are in love?"

"Yes," Di nodded.

"Phew, that's a relief. Now I can stop worrying that you'll hit on me."

Di looked at me, I glanced back. The corners of her mouth were resisting a smile, teeth biting her lip in case laughter was the wrong choice. My glance was quick because I, too, was unsure of the decorum expected when two friends discover they've just been transported to another reality. Di looked out her side window; I kept my eyes on the road. A brief silence ensued — very brief — then, simultaneously, we lost it. I laughed so loud I scared myself. Di laughed out her nose and had to scramble for a napkin in the glove box. I started gagging as I had a weak stomach where snot was concerned. Diane roared, I snorted. I could barely see to drive and had slowed down to only 40 miles an hour. Fortunately, traffic was light and the rest stop directly ahead. We pulled over to the side of the off ramp; I could go no further.

"You are such a #@$%^ liar," Di blurted between laughs. We both knew that I was shocked by what she had told me. We both knew that I was — or at least had been the entire time we knew me — a homophobe.

"You should have seen your face," I blurted between breaths and laughter.

"My face?" Di squealed, "You were trying so hard to be cool about it that you looked like your mother."

"You have never met my mother."

"I have now."

We laughed until our jaws hurt.

And that was it. How in the world could I stop loving my friend because she was in love with another woman? She wasn't a sick, depraved, lost soul. She was still everything I ever loved and admired about her — and by the way, she was in love with another woman. So what! She had been in love with Mary the entire two years I had known her — and now what? Was I supposed to think about her differently? I couldn't do it. What I had been taught, and never questioned as a simple sad fact of life, had just been in a head-on collision with someone I loved.

The general understanding in our world is that it takes a lot of time and hard work to shift a paradigm. Well, that in itself is a paradigm, not a truth. In less than a moment, I changed a strongly held paradigm in my own life. *It is easy to say I must never have believed what I had been taught in the first place.* Not true. I more than believed it, it was a known fact of life. I thought homosexuality was sick, sick, sick. I had been one of those people to feel sorry for effeminate boys and dike-like girls, but never befriended them. So how did I do it? How did I make up my mind so quickly and so absolutely? Was I just faking it, trying to avoid conflict? Did I discover later that it really did bother me? It wasn't that complicated, nor was it anything heroic. All I knew in that moment was: I loved Diane. She was my loyal, supportive, playful friend, and I was hers. End of story.

Our conversation had been revealing in more ways than the obvious. The life I thought I lived did not exist, it was an illusion. My year of no dating was not because I was undesirable — it was because everyone knew I was lesbian — everyone but me of course. Betty, coach's best friend of more than twenty years, was not just a roommate but the love of her life. Teresa and Cindy weren't just affectionate teammates — they were lovers. My weekly dancing buddies were not just women who would rather dance than wait for a man to ask them, they had no desire to dance with men — at least not straight men. Oh, and that night, a few months prior, when Karen asked me if I'd ever kissed a girl, and I said, "Of course, I am very affectionate" — then I leaned over and kissed Mary on the cheek and gave her a big hug? I was thinking Karen maybe, possibly, probably, was hitting on me. I turned to Di and asked: "Are all my friends gay?"

Diane said, "Pretty much".

"Ken?" I asked.

"He is as gay as they come and so are Jim and Jesse." Di confirmed. Silence dropped for a moment and then the laughter returned. My life was now officially inside out and the seams were showing. I learned that I was considered a fag-hag by some and a closeted lesbian by others. I had even been the subject of conversations about whether I was a lipstick or a dike – it seems I fit both. Whomever I seemed to be to others, or thought I was to the world – was obviously out of my control.

The last fifty miles home altered my mind. I'd made a profound step upon my journey of discovering who I am rather than who I was raised to be — and I liked me much better. I liked who I was as a friend. I realized that I knew how to love. I felt an immovable, almost stubborn strength in my love. It gave me security, confidence and a kind of authority over my life I never knew I had lacked. I also became aware of how imprisoned I was by my judgments. I had lived so long behind my bars of quiet self-righteousness that I no longer saw them. I'd forgotten they existed. I am confident no child is born with prejudice, yet I had been raised with it and had long ago forgotten my natural state of acceptance. I didn't know how much of life I'd missed while creating a home in my little cell of narrow-mindedness. I didn't even know there was a world outside that prison, I thought that cell was the world. When love showed up, unlocked and opened the door — I walked.

Admittedly I walked in heels more often and with more hip action when I passed guys. I walked up to Ken and laid a full lipped, enticing kiss on him and said, "Hags need love too." He smiled and patted my butt as we walked to class. I walked confidently out on that dance floor every Saturday with my friends and had a blast. Karen got her kiss and we all agreed I had not been living in a closet about my sexual preference, just enslaved by my ignorance. Somehow my visual priorities changed. I no longer looked at people to make a decision about them; rather I looked for their hidden magic. I figured if one of my best friends could keep from me a major part of who she was for two years then: a) I lacked observational skills and was obviously too self-involved, and, b) my narrow-mindedness had shut my eyes to some pretty great people and I was now ready to see. I had not been living in a closet about my sexuality, enslaved by my ignorance, yes — but straight none the less.

In that one moment of my twenty-year-old life, I chose love. By choosing love in that moment I came to understand it in an entirely new light. Love was no longer a word or an emotion to me. Love was a power beyond anything I could ever fully understand. I knew the more I chose love, the more I would see life, and since life is eternal, then so is love. No matter what I would ever face in life, all I had to remember was to choose love. If I simply and always chose love, my questions would be answered with love, my troubles would be resolved with love, and my life would be filled with love. This was a big revelation for my twenty-year-old mind — one that would serve me for the rest of my life.

Retelling Your Stories

THE MORALS AND BELIEFS WE ARE BROUGHT UP WITH are filled with inherited stories. We know this because they change from culture to culture. Your steadfast beliefs of right and wrong would not be the same if you had been raised in a different society. When we do grow in consciousness and self awareness, we often discover we no longer agree with what our "elders" taught us. Additionally, when we disagree, we think it is our job to argue our side. It doesn't work, but we keep doing it expecting a different result. People do not need agreement, they need understanding. Any separation you have between yourself and another is an announcement to wake up and listen — not to garner ammo for a fight, but to seek understanding. This simple act can change a world of conflict.

I.   What are some of your morals or values that have changed? Can you remember how unquestionably you held a belief that has now changed? Create a story about how that happened and how it enriched your life.

2. Take a look at something you have argued about lately. Identify the value, moral or standard you were defending. Now take the other side and defend the other person's view. You can also ask the other person to argue with you about it — each taking the other person's side until you both feel understood.

3. What are a few of your most passionate opinions? Take a look at political, cultural, religious, relationship and/or health issues.

   a. Now tell a story from the view of the other side. This story must be as high in integrity, as honest, positive and "good" as one told from your own point of view. Give proof with your points.

4. We all like to think we are great listeners but few are. When you realize you are not listening, step back, release your know-it-all attitude, regroup and seek **only** to understand the other person.

On The Edge

There is no agony like bearing an untold story inside of you.
~ Maya Angelou

By the age of twenty-five I was rolling in the dough. Money was an easy thing for me to make and a fun thing for me to spend and give away. I was at the top of my game and one of the best in my business. This is not surprising since I had begun my craft at the age of five and honed it over the years. One might well call me an entrepreneur, and I guess I could tell the story with that twist. I, however, will use the more common occupational title for my work: I was a thief, a con.

I am not speaking metaphorically. I stole for a living. I had a legitimate cover job, for which I would win many awards over the years and eventually, would take me into legal entrepreneurship. I liked my legit job; it paid well. I liked who I was in the position I held. It was a job that asked me to listen to the needs of people and to see if I could give them what they needed, and if not — to help direct them to someone who could. I was a salesperson. You may think that being a con is synonymous with being a salesperson. Perhaps there is some truth to that idea, but only if a person is bad at either. Unfortunately and fortunately — I excelled at both.

My profession as a thief was based on many "facts" I garnered from my youth. Although at age twenty-five, I had healed some of the beliefs in these areas, the "high" from stealing still felt good against the skin of my unworthiness and lack of lovability. My self awareness still possessed dregs of believing I was stupid, ugly, unlovable, with no one but myself to depend upon. As a child, when I would steal it made me feel intelligent. It also made me feel special, and helped me to dress more in style and thus feel more accepted at school. When I would steal, I felt less vulnerable to the world. I knew I could better handle the grownup problems in which we children of single parents are often included. Additionally, conning others showed me I could be tough, determined and persuasive. I also discovered a talent I had inherited from my father — I could see behind the masks of others. I could spot a store detective a mile away. I could tell if a person was unhappy even when they were smiling and laughing. I could sense loneliness, doubt, and frustration often before the individual knew it and I would feed that. I would make them feel better and I would feel better.

By the time I was twelve, simple shoplifting became a bore. I tried stealing from a friend and discovered I hated that. When I was thirteen, I caught on to something. I found it simple to be the kind of young teen adults would trust. At a large local department store, I made a point to get to know all the clerks. I slowly, unassumingly created an image as an industrious, pleasant and hardworking young lady — willing to help them out, even if they couldn't pay me. I explained that I had a very difficult situation with a stepfather at home and needed a place where I would be safe until he drank himself to sleep — a total fabrication by the way. I told my story masterfully, they believed it completely. That year I had a new stylish wardrobe for school — a critical factor to middle school success. This was also the year I got the bug for philanthropy. I would look for women, usually with children, who were struggling. I would watch them and listen to them, making note of what they wanted versus what they could afford. Then I would get their addresses off of their checks, lift the things I knew they wanted and leave them at their door. This took a lot more planning, skill and execution — raising my self-esteem. With this "success" a new fact entered my mind: all I have to do is get people's trust and I can get anything I want from them. And so began my ten-year criminal career.

How could I possibly do this to people who trusted me? It was easy. I was thoughtless, self-centered, cocky, cruel, dishonest, alone and unworthy — I was exactly what I knew myself to be. During my ten-year jaunt on the dark side, I kept up a great front. I received scholarships and awards for academia, bookkeeping, improvisation, mime, basketball, dance, volleyball and track. I was on The Dean's List, in Honor Society, and a Phi Beta Kappa. I had an image of being hard-working, kind, intelligent, fun-loving, trustworthy and courageous. I was seen as the "All-American Girl next door with a wonderful future." In my mind I was a con. No one knew who I really was, and no one ever could.

Every human is multi-faceted in their expression of life. Even though television has convinced us that there are only white or black-hatted characters in the world, the truth is, there are endless colors and shades of character within every person. I can say nothing to change the "dark" side of my character — but that doesn't mean it is the only hue in my being.

When I was twenty-four-years of age, I was flying high as a sales person for an internationally known company in the health and beauty aid industry. I was making good money as a rising star in the corporate world. I owned my home, drove a hot car and had a terrific boyfriend — all obtained honestly with money I had earned. I was living a second life continuing to play out elaborate cons. There is little I can say to make myself appear to have had a conscious or decent morality in these years. The only boundary I seemed to have was to not steal from someone who I thought needed what was taken. I pretty much liked to see myself as a kind of Robin Hood. I understand now that I was just conning myself. In my found love for giving money to charity, I actually won city and state awards for my philanthropy. How sick is that?

One day I decided I wanted a new summer ensemble for my upcoming trip to Acapulco, and I thought it would be entertaining not to pay for it. I was to be honored as Sales Person of the Year by my company. I went into a large clothing store and I lifted an entire wardrobe, totaling several hundreds of dollars. I then walked into a jewelry store and got what I wanted there — that was a thrill. My final stop was at a tall shop. I was looking for a couple of long, feminine summer dresses for the anticipated hot Mexico nights of dancing.

When I walked out of the door, two men grabbed hold of each of my arms and asked me to come with them. I had never been caught stealing anything, not even the proverbial bubble gum when I was a tot. That does not mean I had not planned for such an occasion. I calmly went with the security guards. When the police arrived I was taken away, arrested and finger printed for grand theft. I easily paid cash for my first offense bail and returned home where I instantly called the person at the *Oregonian* I had come to know for just such an occasion. I convinced him to leave my name out of the paper if such news passed his desk. Then I called my attorney, another acquired friend with ulterior motives. It was quite simple to convince both men that I was the victim in this situation.

I prepared for the court date as any con would. I dressed the part of the All-American Girl. The dress had white background behind soft pink, yellow and green flowers, a touch of lace at the collar and sleeves. My shoes were flat white, prissy things ornamented with the proverbial bow. I had my hair cut and softly highlighted to exaggerate my natural girl-next-door appearance and wore light make up. The whole look was perfect — I embodied the quintessential sweet daughter every one thought existed in the world. I walked into the courtroom in full character — this would be one of the most successful cons of my life. As the judge entered, we all stood. One look at him, and I bowed my head, a tear rolling down my cheek without permission and against my will.

That day, the judge — I will call him the honorable Jonathan Randall Twain — knew me. He knew me in a very special way. I remained with my eyes down until my case was called. I walked to the table with my attorney and sat down. Robed and staring intently down at me from the bench was the father of a young man whose life I had saved the previous year — or so his honor seemed to think.

I had been a volunteer for *Teens on the Edge* for a couple of years. I really liked working with young people who at any moment could become leaders in society or leaders in the joint; I wonder why? The son of Judge Jon was in pretty deep trouble when I met him. He was an alcoholic, unable to go more than a couple of hours without drinking. He had been caught stealing a car and vandalizing federal property. Jonathan Jr. (J.J.) had joined *Teens on the Edge* at the insistence of his father. The judge had heard some things about me and specifically requested that I work with his son. I found J.J. to be an amazing young man. He was clever, funny, resourceful, and I could see a true empathy in him. He carried different self-facts in his brain of course. J.J. and I met when he was just out of detox — we hit it off. I found it quite easy to support him in better choices. We became close and I visited his family several times. Judge Jon decided that my faith in J.J. was the key in turning his life around.

The judge I was facing was a man who believed that I had a lot of good to offer this world. Judge Jon was having difficulty with what he saw in that court room that day. His first words were, "Did you do this?" "Yes," I said looking straight into his eyes. I was looking into eyes that had discovered my shadow, my darkness, and I wanted to watch as those eyes changed from caring to disappointment and disgust. "Then you have probably done this before." He returned my intensity. Then I saw it. There in the eyes of this gentle giant of a man I saw sorrow. He was concerned for me. "Yes, I have," I said with strength and some weird sense of honor.

Following a short conversation between the legal entities in the room — none of which I recall — I found myself alone in Judge Jon's chambers. He had a few things he wanted to know from me. He wanted to know how long I had been stealing. He asked details about when, what, how. I kept my eyes up, my voice steady, and told

him everything. I kept waiting for him to ask me why —
he never did. After what memory tells me was forever, he
stopped the questions. He turned in his chair, stared out
of the window and said he had one more question to ask
me. "I sense such sadness and loneliness in you that I
never saw before, yet I have seen no tears. Do you feel
remorse for the life you have lived?" He turned to face
me, awaiting my response.

My eyes puddled and he rose from his chair, walked
around to embrace me. I stiff-armed him; I was angry. I
had decided I would not use tears to manipulate this man
I admired. Steadying my voice I reported, "Tears melt the
toughest and most clever of men when you use them
right," I dabbed my eyes. "Don't fall for it, your Honor."

He tossed his eyes to the ceiling and let out a soft
chuckle. "I suppose," he said, "those words could be the
ultimate con, but I don't believe it." Then he looked at me
with what I had always imagined were fatherly eyes. With
a genuine smile of pride he told me, "It is rare to have the
privilege of meeting as honest, compassionate and
beautiful a soul as you. Tell me that you will never steal
again and I will believe you."

Facts were colliding in my head and making a
terrible pile-up. My reality was going up in flames. Fact:
I was a good liar. Fact: I see people for who they really
are, not who they pretend to be. Fact: Judge Jon is a
genuine human being, sharp, intelligent and not easily

fooled. I trust him. Fact: I am unworthy, dishonest, a trouble maker. Fact: He knew my darkness and yet appeared to still like me. Crash: What was going on? Was I wrong about who he was? That didn't compute. Was he manipulating me? That didn't fit either. Could I be what he thought I was?

In my colored past I had learned the value of letting go. When the unexpected starts happening, you have to release attachment to the plan and the outcome and go with your gut. My gut believed this man. I looked into his eyes for a long time. I would make the promise only if I could keep it. I whispered, "I'm not sure how to live without stealing; I have done it for most of my life."

He responded, "Promise me, and I will believe you."

I put my face in my hands and thought hard. Finally I looked up into those waiting unforgettable eyes and said, "I don't know how to quit."

He wrote down the name of a professional who he believed could help me, and I left the court room that day sentenced to three years community service, assigned to work with *Teens on the Edge.*

That afternoon I went to Dr. Mower. I saw him for three years, once a week. I went to him with cemented, absolute facts in my head about my self, others, society and life in general — all of which justified my being a con and thief.

The mind is a powerful force. When the mind

decides a thing is true, it takes great faith to change it. I did not know how to change my mind, but I had faith that others did. It was all I knew how to do. I had faith in my doctor and in Judge Jon. I had faith that they were good people who wanted to help me. It was during these years that I discovered those "facts" in my head that had made me who I was. Before that, I was unconscious about who I was and why I did what I did. It never occurred to me that life was the accumulation of "facts" I chose to believe. Now I knew it was possible to change my mind. Reason, logic or proof would not get me there, so I let go of the how and the outcome. I chose faith as my means.

I would not have labeled myself a person of trust or faith until I was called up to drastically turn my life around. Looking back, I found examples of where I had trusted and put faith in others. I had come through an irrecoverable paralysis, earned a four-year degree and became a dynamic business woman — all while the facts in my head told me none of that was possible. Somehow, in the living of my double life, I had created relationships of love, support, compassion and devotion. Nothing "factual" in my self-view could explain that. I simply had to believe it was true — and then of course, it was. Surrounding me in my world were amazingly generous and accepting people. When they found out about my past, they didn't care. They asked a lot of questions but not a one of them turned his back on me.

During the past twenty-five years I continued to question my facts and stayed willing to change my mind. I have discovered that when a person is defensive it is because he/she is protecting a fact. The minute I hear myself doing this, I open my mind to other views and other truths. The four years before this wake-up call I had attempted to change my mind through books, exercises and seminars by "experts." I would usually feel better after completing any one of them. I would "share" with others the great new truth or ways I had discovered. Rarely did any of this change the "facts" that were shading my reality. Judge Jon brought to my awareness the unparalleled catalyst of faith and trust. I began to see the ludicrous habit we humans have of trying to resolve troubles from the same mind that created them in the first place. Letting go with faith allows new thoughts, ideas and facts to enter the mind, creating fresh solutions, possibilities and hope. It also helps recognize when an angel enters your life — judge or no.

Retelling Your Story

EVERYBODY HAS GOOD IN THEM. EVERYBODY! YOU CAN argue with me, prove I am wrong — but that's your story and I am sticking to mine. No matter how thoughtless, cruel, crooked, dishonest, conniving or devious a person may be — there is good inside somewhere. Even in you, or I should say especially in you. Inside of you glows a light of wonder beyond your imagination, and the way to find it is not with more light, but by walking into the darkness.

We humans have a habit of labeling things "good" or "bad." This black and white pattern of life hinders our happiness, honesty, prosperity and relationships. Worrying about what others think creates an excessive waste of energy. A waste because what another thinks of you, really has nothing to do with you — and is none of your business.

I.   Create a melodramatic horror story of you revealing your deepest, darkest uglies to those you love most in the world. Consider shames, fears, cruelties, deceptions, lapses of integrity, unspoken opinions and embarrassments. Imagine your beloveds reacting in the most horrifyingly awful way you can imagine.

2. Now consider what the logical reaction would be if you revealed your darkest secrets?

3. Finally, retell your "confession" as a love story. Realize the acceptance, notice the closeness that occurs and witness your own lack of defensiveness.

4. When the story feels good, when it feels real to you, tell it to a neutral party. A therapist is a great choice and fellow members of a 12-step program can provide a good ear as well.

5. The time will come to tell loved ones, and finally to tell the world — without apology or shame. When the world is blessed by your story, you become a healer to all who have not yet opened their own closet of darkness.

6. Repeat this process with anything that for any reason you feel needs to remain hidden.

Untangled Web

Loneliness haunted me; freedom evaded me — until I accepted my freedom to fail.

~ Teri Hawkins

I USED TO WISH I WOULD HAVE THE GREAT GIFTS I SAW others getting. Like my friend who got $25,000 to travel the world for a year before entering college — I really coveted that gift. Then there were all the times that I would witness women getting great jewelry, wonderful days at a spa, or surprise trips to romantic, tropical getaways. I had come to realize I was just someone who would never get gifts like that. I wasn't pretty enough, interesting enough, or deserving enough. All that changed when, in my early thirties, I received a gift I did not even know was available — and I received it on one of the worst days of my life.

This magnificent gift came from a woman named Dianna. She was the regional sales manager for Dale Carnegie. We had brushed by one another in the professional world of Portland, not knowing much more than each other's name and rank. I knew people who knew her and vise versa. She came to my store a couple of times and we shook hands briefly at a few events. When my store's name was purchased by a major retailer, I was ready to be a full-time professional speaker and trainer. Somewhere in that transition Dianna and I began to talk. She was ready to leave Carnegie. Her greatest dream was to be the person behind someone who made a difference in the world. My greatest dream was to be that person who made a difference in the world. We became partners in business. It seemed a perfect fit on the surface, but like a beautiful mountain lake, the majority of our connection was much deeper than any visible surface might reflect.

As we were putting together our partnership I blew it big time. I did something that I knew was unforgivable. I knew it would be over between us. I had presented a proposal to a good-size, family-owned business. I lined up all the reference letters, my resume and bio were sharp, and I had outlined what I could do to create teamwork and increase employee dedication to the company vision. I'd won the contract and for the first two months they were ecstatic about the results. Everything was blooming for me in the Rose City.

While in a session training on goal setting, I told a story about how I had always wanted to be an Olympic athlete, and that just as I'd made the team, the Olympics were boycotted. A man in the audience looked up the names of the Olympic volleyball team in 1980 and did not find mine among them. He reported this to the CEO of the company who although not terribly upset about the story, decided to check up on all the references I had given him. It started out fine, no problem. Everything checked out, except for the final two letters of reference, which I had altered from dull letters of recommendation to glorious letters touting my unparalleled skills and genius.

I was called into the office and found myself on the wrong side (as if there could ever be a right side) of an inquisition. I was shamed, horrified and discredited.

These people liked me, liked my work and what I had done to lead their company in a new direction. That was all over. I was fired the first and only time in my life. The people who actually had recommended me (for real) were called and told that I was dishonest and had lied. I remember thinking I would have to move from Portland and that my professional life was over.

As much as I wanted to soft-soap it with Dianna, she had to be told. If given a choice that day I would have preferred a root canal without anesthesia. I knew Dianna and I were through and the pain of that loss would be with me for life. Although we were not yet in full partnership, we had become dear friends. Dianna had already given me a present I'd dreamed about my entire life, yet never felt worthy of receiving. She'd given me a loving family.

Dianna was raised in a home of devotion, hard work, support and unquestionable loyalty. She is that kind of mother and wife as well. Her two sons were nine and thirteen when we met and I fell in love with both in minutes. Cliff, Dianna's husband, is one of the best fathers I have ever witnessed in life. It was into this family that I was welcomed. We shared Thanksgiving, Christmas, big family get-togethers; I played Bunko with Di's mom, went to the boys games, heard about every day trials and became a part of them. Now, due to my own lack of integrity and falsifications (a pretty word for "lies") I would lose this family I'd grown to love and a friend who could have been for life. Still, I had to tell her before someone else did. She had brought me into the sanctuary of her home, trusted her professional career to me, and offered me the very support I'd always wanted. I was going to return the favor by betraying her, hurting her family and turning her life upside down. I wanted to disappear, but I owed her more than that.

I will never forget telling her. I have a powerfully strong physical reaction that returns every time I think about it, even now more than twenty years later. I told Dianna as directly and honestly as I could what had happened, trying to present some sort of integrity or honor. But she would have none of it. Her response was devastating! Not to me. Not to her. Not to our partnership. It was devastating to who I had been. It was the kind of life-leveling devastation that creates space for new growth. My old life died that day as a new one began.

What was this wise, life-changing response she gave me? Well, she looked at me and asked if I wanted her to go back and clear out the on-site office. Huh? You have got to be kidding! I looked, but there was not a smidgen of accusation or even disappointment to be found in her eyes, voice or posture. It was for real. She simply acknowledged I had made a mistake and offered to help diminish my suffering. It was the perfect definition of a surreal moment. I had no point of reference to help me understand what was happening. I was looking into the eyes of someone who wasn't going anywhere — except over to clean out my office so I would have no further shame to bear.

Within a life of theft, one will always find a pack of lies. I had stopped stealing years before, but the practice of lying had not yet found its way out of my habits. Lies are the stories we tell to make ourselves look better or worse than we actually are. All forms of lies come from low self-acceptance and the lack of self-love. My image was respected by others, but no one really knew who I was. I protected the shadow side of my personality because I was so sure no one would want anything to do with me if they knew. Now this clear, warm light of love was shining on that darkness I'd hidden for so long. The very trust and respect I worked so hard for had evaded me, because I had never felt I could be completely me. I had created an endless spiral down into a deepening hole of loneliness. My rabbit hole had more twists and turns in it than a Midwestern tornado. I had no visible way out of the isolation I'd created. Now beside me was a friend illuminating my escape.

Dianna had in that critical moment been Dianna. She did not face a choice to trust me or not, support me or not, love me or not — she'd made that choice already. Dianna did not choose to love the *me* I wanted people to see — she chose to love the *me* I was — including all my human deficits and irritations. She had given me her trust and never considered taking it back because it was no longer hers to take. It was mine to do with what I wished, and for the past twenty years I have cherished that gift with all my heart. At times it gets dusty from lack of use, but never does it lose its strength or inner luster.

With my background one might think Di was a bit naïve in trusting me. Yet, I am the one who handled the money in our partnership. I personally think she was a genius. It ends up I am a very loyal, devoted and trustworthy friend — something that seems incongruous with my past. I discovered this the day the world as I knew it crumbled into useless rubble, and the rich, full life I dreamed of began.

Because she saw a loving, giving, trustworthy person in me — I became that in the world. It took years for me to totally stop the need to impress others by exaggerating who I was or what I had done. Eventually I created a life filled with happenings, loved ones, and self acceptance that erased my need to be more. Through it all Di loved and trusted me neither more, nor less, than when she first gave me her friendship. It is a gift that keeps on giving through the trust I have been able to give unconditionally to others.

Whatever I do that makes a difference in this world, I do because someone loved me for who I was and gave me the gift of trust. It was in this gift that I learned trust can never be lost. It's a gift that is given, and once given, is no longer yours to take back. If you do take it back, it is because you never really gave it. Trust does not have a line that, if crossed, disenfranchises you from the person who gave it. Trust does not exist if it comes with conditions. Certainly we all choose to whom we wish to give our gifts, and whether they are priceless in dollars or in life, once we receive them they are ours to do with what we will.

The best gift I was ever given was the realization that I am good — even with my not so good stuff — that I am loved with all my flaws, that I am a devoted friend who can be trusted, trusts back and knows what loyalty is from a deep core of understanding. Dianna, in giving me trust, gave me — Me. This means that everything I have given the world, or will give the world since that moment — she is behind.

Retelling Your Story

Giving is a powerfully spiritual experience. When we give we become a part of the flow of life itself. One can never give too much — nor give more than received. Giving is a powerful energy that creates miracles of abundance in the life of every human who understands it. If you lack abundance in any area, then basically, you are not giving in that area.

We are not raised to understand giving. We are raised to meet obligations, sacrifice wants, impress others and expect certain reactions. When we give a gift because we are supposed to; when we sacrifice to give to another; when we give with attachment to how the receiver will like or appreciate our gift — that is not giving.

When we give a thing it is no longer ours, so what another does with it is really none of our business. If we give out of duty we are giving with expectations of appreciation. When we are under the illusion that we give more than we receive, we are giving to create an image, a reputation — and that is not giving.

The greatest giving we do in life has nothing to do with holidays, birthdays, wrapping paper, bows or large price tags. Our best gifts are the smiles we give out daily, the love we give freely, the laughter we share openly and the trust we offer completely. None of these can be taken back. If your smile creates a warm smile in return; if you love someone you will always love them; if you laugh and it tickles another — you can not take it back. And, if you give your trust only after it is earned, then it is not a gift at all — it's a payment. If you do give your trust then it is no longer yours to take back. That is the flow you set your life in when you relearn true giving.

1. Write down all the places and times you can remember when you have given out of obligation, to avoid bad feelings, or because you would feel discomfort if you didn't give.

2. Create a list of things you would love that do not cost a penny. Do this with family, friends and/or work associates. Brainstorm on nice things you can do, adventures you can take, games you can play, things you can create, compliments you can give, stories you can share. Give from this list at birthdays and holidays. See what you learn about giving and notice changes in your feelings of prosperity and happiness.

3. Make note of stories that come from any of this.

The Audacious Seagull

If you are going to jump off a cliff, do it to soar, not to fall.
If someone pushes you off the cliff, just spread your wings.
                                                    ~ Teri Hawkins

THERE ARE CERTAIN PLACES IN LIFE WHERE HEAVEN IS easy to find. There's the magnificent beauty of nature and the glorious laughter of friends, but one of my favorite heavenly experiences happens in a car. Not just any car, a car that likes to drive rather than ride. I find a high performance machine euphoric. A standard transmission provides the opportunity for common prayer between me and the car — we hear each other and respond support-ively. A quality stereo system raises me up to a higher awareness, add a soft top and I am through the gates, leaving St. Peter in angel dust. One day, while driving my highway to heaven north along the Oregon Coast, we pulled over — *we* being one of my all time favorite cars and I.

The sun had been active in its shining all day and now it was getting ready for bed. We had come to a place where you can sit on the edge of a cliff and see nothing but ocean meeting sky. It is one of those secret places that native Oregonians always seem to forget to tell tourists about.

I am partial to cliffs; they make takeoff easier when we are called to fly. We are all born to fly, each equipped with the wings needed to glide on the winds of life. Personal interpretations of various experiences may clip our wings for a while or fold them under, out of sight — but they are still there. When the time comes to soar, I suggest we head for a cliff. We work through childhood traumas and take responsibility for our life, getting ever closer to that cliff. We begin to strip emotional weight from our wings and dream of all the possibilities in our life, seeing the edge of the overhang. We see others fly, identify our own dreams, and realize our turn to soar is coming soon. With toes hanging over the very edge of the precipice, we look down and see a jagged bedrock of doubts, what-ifs and fears. Friends and family call to us, not wanting us to fall and hurt ourselves. Their concern causes us to back away from the edge. Yet life is a strong wind beneath our wings, reminding us of our dreams. We again walk to the edge. We try our wings and feel a supporting lift, but remain attached to the known comfort of earth. We want to fly but how do we take that first step?

Here is where my life work comes in; I love to push people off that edge. That may seem aggressive, but it is the most loving, unselfish thing I have ever done for another person. I push people off their cliff because I know they can fly. They may not yet know it — but I have no doubts. I do not take others for rides when I fly, nor am I a flight instructor. I used to think I was, until I realized every person is so aerodynamically different that no one can teach another to fly. Besides, we all instinctively know all on our own. There was a time when I tried coaxing, inspiring, coercing and even bribing people off the edge. Then I asked myself: *Why not just push them. It seems rude, but if I believe in them, then there is no downside to pushing. If I don't believe in them — then I shouldn't be teaching people to follow their dreams.* Yep, I am quite partial to cliffs.

So I was sitting on the edge of this cliff overlooking the wide Pacific, as the ocean surface began to turn into Bach-water — a name I give water when it turns reflective silver. I am a big fan of Richard Bach, the author of a book I count amongst my all-time favorites: *Jonathan Livingston Seagull.* Bach has a picture on several of his books of a small engine plane flying over silver water — thus the invention of the term Bach-water. Sitting there, enjoying the changing light, I began to hear the sound of a small engine plane. I scanned the horizon, turned 360 degrees searching for the source of the sound. *It must be something else,* I thought. The sound persisted. I was sure it was a plane.

Uncharacteristically, I began to get irritated. Why couldn't I find that plane? Where was it? Was this some kind of cosmic joke? Was there a Bach-message trying to get through to me? The moment that thought came to me, a seagull landed a mere two feet away. He stood still and we stared into each other's eyes. I laughed inside. Sarcastically I said, "Jonathan, I presume?" He took two steps toward me, never removing his eyes from mine. "Okay," I said, enjoying the cartoon, "What's up?"

If you have a bit of the practical or a tad of the skeptical in you, then perhaps you are saying some of the same things I was saying to myself:

What is the big deal about a seagull landing next to you when you are sitting on a cliff above the ocean? There are seagulls everywhere on the Oregon Coast. So he stepped toward you when you talked? He probably is used to people feeding him and just thought you were going to oblige. No big deal about a plane. On a beautiful day private pilots go up all the time, especially at this time of day, and the silver water is just the reflection of sunlight out of a blank sky.

I said all of that to myself and I meant it. It was what the gull did next that changed my life. He turned, walked to the edge, stood for a moment looking and hopped off the cliff. He fell out of my sight for a few moments and then in the distant, now silent sky, I saw him. Silhouetted by the lazy light of the sun, he was dancing on the wind.

When the student is ready, the teacher will appear. I know that to be true, for too often people have credited me for something they have learned — not possible. If we open our minds and are willing to learn, we learn. What I learn is up to no one but me. When that bird dropped from the cliff I was horrified, because simultaneously he had also hung my toes over the most imposing metaphoric cliff I'd ever approached in my life. Having jumped off these kinds of cliffs before, one would think each one would get easier. I mean, once you know you can fly, what's the big deal? This cliff was so high I could not see the rocks below. It was so high that gale-force winds grabbed at me, ready to toss me about. I was convinced I lacked the experience to navigate from this height.

I had heard stories from people who had taken a path to that incredible height — none of them enticed me. I had never pushed someone from this cliff, maybe subconsciously knowing it contained winds I was unwilling to deal with.

My cliff of fear was ministry. I was not a minister. I was not a religious person; I was a spiritual person. I did not want to be a part of the dogma that had separated people from one another. *No! No! No!* I stepped back from the overhang, got in my car, put up the top, turned off the stereo and cruised into Newport, the next town.

It was Sunday and I was expected at a Halloween party I was obviously going to miss. I called Dianna to tell her not to expect me. Dianna knew me better than anyone. She "got me." During my call to her I mentioned, "You would not believe what happened this weekend." With a laugh for the ludicrous I continued, "A lady asked me if I had ever thought of being a minister. What a joke, huh?"

I chuckled, Dianna didn't. I had called her knowing that she would draw me back from the edge of that cliff. When she spoke, it was with sincerity:

"It's perfect! That's what you have always wanted to be."

WHAT? It is not what I always wanted to be. I have

never even thought of being a minister. I called another friend, someone who was business savvy. He loved money, prestige and respected my business success. He understood that I loved my work and was living my dream. Bob would see the illogical and the impractical aspects of ministry. He would assure me that I could talk at a church anytime I wanted with no need to leave my business and do it full time. He answered the phone. We chatted a moment about nothing, then I slipped in the aside, "A lady I met this weekend asked me if I ever thought of being a minister. A minister?"

You know when you say to someone, "How are you doing?" and they say, "Fine!" You know that tone when they say "fine" — that kind of automatic, over-practiced tone that lacks attachment? Well it was in this tone that Bob said,

"Sounds like a good idea."

He was either sidetracked or he was mad at me, and knowing how I dislike passive-aggressive behavior, was saying it just to be irritating. Granted, Bob had never used this skill before, but, well. . . I called Tina.

Tina possesses unique dichotomies in her personality. She can make a cohesive team out of intellectual, analytical computer geeks who prefer autonomy; while — unbeknownst to them — she has all kinds of crystals in her bra for various New Age reasons. Tina has always loved to watch me fly and has been my wind countless times. In hindsight, I guess I knew what she would say, but the clouds surrounding me on that cliff blinded me.

Her response, "I'm not surprised; you'll be great at that!"

Three months later, I was driving my car down to Coos Bay, following a U-Haul loaded with all my possessions. The Association of Unity Churches had come up with an agreement so that I could be the minister with "special dispensation" as long as I agreed to take a certain number of classes at Unity Village in Kansas City, Missouri. I had jumped, and I was managing the air currents fairly well. I was still high above the clouds unable to see the ground, but I was holding up just fine. Then, without warning, I hit a storm inside myself that put me into a tailspin. I was informed that Unity followed the teachings of Jesus.

This benevolent, gentle group of people had shown faith in me and hired me to be their spiritual leader (a name I was much more comfortable with than *minister*). You would have thought that somewhere in the interviewing process, sometime in the previous three months, someone would have mentioned that Unity used the *Bible* as a source for its teachings.

I was in a conundrum. My integrity was important to me as a leader. I could never be everything everyone wanted me to be, but I could be true to who I was. I was a person who believed the *Bible* had been used to justify war, murder, abuse and bigotry. I was a person who believed the *Bible* needed to be removed from society. I was against almost everything I had heard about the *Bible*. When it came to Jesus — I had no relationship with him. For as long as I could remember, I was repulsed by the thought of worshipping a tortured soul nailed to a cross. It seemed like an open invitation for people to live in guilt and deny responsibility for their lives. My only memory of Jesus in childhood was a picture my grand-mother had in her living room. He was alive in that picture and happily surrounded by sweet lambs and angelic children. This was my relationship with Jesus and the *Bible*, and I was now the minister of a church that followed the teachings of Jesus and referred to the *Bible* for spiritual support. Oops! Now what?

I called Unity headquarters and registered for the *Bible* Overview class. Then I got in my car, put down the top and took a long drive south on the coastal highway. Just out of town I turned on the stereo. Celine Dion was singing:

Fly, fly little wing,
Fly beyond imagining

Retelling Your Story

A whisper is one of the best ways in the world to get someone's attention. Typically, we humans resort to raising the voice instead of lowering it. Life is different. Life understands that loud demands create defensiveness while the quiet whisper reels a person in slowly but surely.

Let's look at telling some quiet stories.

I. Create a peaceful, quiet little haven in your home and maybe one at work. Include favorite scents, sounds, colors, textures in your space. It does not have to be in anyway extensive — just peaceful and quiet. Then spend time in the silence. Start with ten minutes at home and five minutes once a day at work. Create a sign that says, "Please Honor The Silence." The sign does not exclude others but sets clear boundaries.

    a. At first just experience the silence.

    b. Eventually increase the time.

    c. The silence will rewrite many stories without effort. It can also find stories that are deeply hidden and are now ready to be retold.

2. Quiet stories can also be insidious. One of the most damaging "quiet" tales is sarcasm. It is a slippery way for people to put down one another, to feel superior. Calling another, or ourself, on sarcasm can be challenging. So lets change our story about this evasive devise of a low self esteem.

    a. List the names of people in your life that use sarcasm, include self on the list — you cannot see something in another that you do not yourself know.

    b. Which of the following do you think they might feel a lack of in their life: appreciation, recognition, safety, understanding, love and/or belonging?

    c. Once you identify a lack start giving it. By giving it to others you will receive it in return. It may feel awkward at first — that is because you are changing a story in midstream. It works!

3. Synchronicity is a quiet yet powerful voice in life. It is the voice that prepares us for change in a gentler way. If we are willing to listen, life is much easier and more enjoyable. Take a look backward at some of the major changes in your life and recall all the little signs that led you toward that change. Were you conscious of all the signs along the way,

or did you wait until you were on the edge of the cliff before you decided to look?

4.   What stories do you have that support the idea that you do not like change? Tell them to yourself. Are they around money or possessions? Safety? Time? Relationships? Responsibility?

a.   First tell the worst case scenario story around a change you are facing.

b.   Now retell the story with you as the courageous hero of a change that is coming and how amazing it is on the other side.

A Better Think Coming

What if our educational systems were to insist that teachers be poets and storytellers and artists? What transformations would follow?

~ Matthew Fox

I HAD FIRST VISITED THE MIDWEST STRAIGHT OUT OF college. I stepped off a vibrating commuter plane onto the tarmac in Cedar Rapids, Iowa. Eyes wide, I began to walk to the terminal. Within a dozen steps my pace had slowed to an unconscious stop. Unbeknownst to me, my trip had been intergalactic. I slowly turned 360 degrees and found nothing blocking the horizon. There were no tall trees, no rolling hills; there were no mountains in the distance. I had never experienced an endless and evasive terrestrial horizon. I felt exposed somehow.

For the entire car ride into Iowa City, I stared out my passenger window, transfixed by the geography. At one point, I excitedly said to my friend, "Amber waves of grain! Look, it's amber waves of grain."

I grew up with purple mountains majesty, but amber waves of grain? I had seen the wheat fields in the Northwest rustling in the breeze, but when the wind blows across Midwestern fields it really looks like rolling waves on the ocean. This realization woke me to new thoughts: *How much do I think I know that I know nothing about? How much is out there that I have no concept even exists? How much of my life and the choices I make are from ignorance about which I'm ignorant?*

As the somewhat too proud, only college graduate in my family, it was a humbling moment for me. With my degree I had adopted a know-it-all attitude without even knowing it. Then I saw those amber waves of grain. In that moment I knew that my knowledge would never be more than a grain of wheat in all the fields and crops of existence. In that moment I became a conscious student of life.

Much of the pull to teach, speak and inspire came from a curiosity to always learn more. I wanted to know more about how people thought, how life created, how things happened, why they didn't, if something was possible and if not, why not? More than anything, I would question what I thought I knew. I would say to myself, *Don't forget, you thought you knew what amber waves of grain were, until you saw them.* Still I would go through the arrogance of arriving, of *already knowing.* I would gather information about things, make my decision and, either aloud or deep within, claim: *I know that!* The *I know* attitude and the *I don't know* attitude are mutually exclusive of each other, yet somehow my ego would convince me that I could be an open-minded know-it-all. How ludicrous is that?

One area I considered myself very open about was religion and spirituality. I hung out with people who agreed with that self-image. I would say, "I honor whatever your path is to higher consciousness." I would listen to all beliefs I ran into. On hot days I gave lemonade to Mormon or Jehovah Witness missionaries who knocked on my door. I would let them say what they needed to say and allow them to pray with me if they asked. I was so open-minded, yet I *knew* a few things about religion. I knew that religion was responsible for a large majority of the separation in humanity. I knew there was too much guilt and shame guiding lives. I knew poverty was not closer to God than wealth. I knew that the masses had given up their ability to think for themselves due to fear of retribution after death. I knew the stories of the *Bible*, the use of the *Bible*, the religions built upon the *Bible* were not something of which any intelligent person would be a part.

I was a big fan of *Lord of the Rings*, not the Lord of the *Bible*. In knowing all this, I saw myself as a part of the solution, rather than the problem. I knew I knew, which meant whoever didn't know what I knew — wasn't in the know. I was so sure I knew that I didn't look at the amber waves of thought trying to reason with me. If I would have listened, I could have heard myself, but I wasn't interested. I would have heard my prejudice, my ignorance. I could have heard that I was a part of the problem. I didn't because I had arrived in a knowing and saw no reason to question it.

Life didn't want me to stagnate, life wanted me to live. So in response to my choice of attitude, life gave me an ultimatum: You can know what you know and defend it as so, or you can be in integrity. You can't have both. Being clearly set in the absolute necessity of an image as a high integrity person, I opted for *I don't know.*

Fifteen years after that first trip to the plains of the Midwest, I returned. This time my ride from the airport was with five exuberant strangers in a limo on our way from Kansas City Airport to Unity Village, Missouri. It became obvious that my general demeanor was different from my companions. While I was hesitant, they were vibrant with anticipation. As I was following duty coming here, they were following passion. Upon arrival at the Village, I discovered my roommate would be Peggy, a passionate, perky, intelligent blonde from Texas. Our room had two desks, each adorned with its own *Bible*. Peggy added a third from her own suitcase. What was I doing here? Had I been snookered? Were they going to try and save me? I prepared myself. I knew I could hold my ground. I knew exactly what the *Bible* was and was not. I knew the closed mindedness of *Bible* thumpers. It might not be a relaxing week, but I would not be swayed by overly enthusiastic Evangelists of the *Bible* or of Christianity. I knew too much to let that happen.

The following morning I found myself walking with a *Bible*-carrying Southern Belle on my way to a *Bible* Overview class. Yeesh! With pride, I reminded myself I was keeping my word. I was being honorable. I was the new spiritual leader of a Unity Church and, after being hired and moving five hours from home, discovered that Unity followed teachings from the *Bible*. I was pretty clear that after this trip, I would probably have to leave due to incompatibility with the teachings – but I would do as I promised to do. I liked thinking I was doing a great thing for those who graced me with trust as a leader. In reality, I was doing everything in my power to prove myself right: I was a person of integrity; I was very well aware of the hypocrisy of the *Bible* and its thumpers; I was a spiritual being, and not a religious puppet. I was right about all of it – so saideth my great knowledge of the time.

I walked into the naturally lit and airy sanctuary of the Silent Unity Chapel and immediately found an inconspicuous chair in which to park myself. I put myself in neutral and waited. I could shift gears as needed.

"So," the instructor began, "what is your opinion of the *Bible*?"

No way would I be speaking up. I am not the sacrificial type.

Immediate responses began flying down the aisle to be written on the chalkboard below. Peggy's was one of the first: "It is a beautiful Book of Truth."

"The *Bible* is filled with mysticism."

"It is an eloquent history of a nomadic people."

Don, the instructor, would nod his head or say, "Yes," and then write it on the huge board for all to see.

Opinions kept coming:

"The *Bible* is the cause of countless deaths and unforgivable suffering."

I turned quickly. Who said that? Was that a plant?

Then: "The *Bible* is sexist and abusive toward women and children."

That one came from the front of the room. I looked at the teacher. He nodded his head, said, "Yes," and wrote it on the board. What was going on?

"The *Bible* is political propaganda written by fathers of the Catholic Church."

"It is a book of beautiful song and poetry."

"It is a library of excuses to destroy anyone who disagrees with you."

"It is a comfort in the darkest of times, a joy to a lonely heart."

"It is a book of lies."

"It is a challenge to know yourself intimately and to love all of you."

"It's a book of love."

"And hatred."

Every thing offered was accepted and written upon a growing list.

I geared up, put my persuasive skills into drive and offered — in my most matter-of-fact voice (or what I now call my know-it-all voice):

"The *Bible* is a piece of literature written by men in the name of their God for political and economic advantage. It was written to control the masses. Through threats of horrific retribution, the writers of the *Bible* convince readers to surrender their individual thought. By doing this, we have created a society of sheep."

Don said, "Yes," and wrote it on the board.

I had put blinders on myself while speaking my truth to the room. I did not want to even glance peripherally at Peggy. I pictured her mouth dropping, horrified at my blasphemy of her HOLY *Bible*. When I had finished speaking I felt a tap on my hand, and Peggy whispered: "Well put!"

Over the years I had traveled extensively using many forms of transportation. Once, I even rode a donkey to get to a remote town in South America. What I had not experienced was the *transporter*. I was so immediately amazed as to what was going on in this room that I was being beamed into another reality. New to the experience, it took my thoughts a few moments to gather back to consciousness.

The opinions went on until we were all out of horrors and beauties to share about the *Bible*. Don then set down his chalk, picked up the *Bible* and said, "All you have said is true. The *Bible* does have dark human history in it; it has many stories never intended to be read as fact; it contains deep mysticism and healing power, it has been used to justify many atrocities and to soothe many souls.

You could tell as he talked that he had a great love for the *Bible*. Yet he was willing to admit it wasn't perfect. His was an unconditional love, without defensiveness around anyone else's opinion. He held up his leather-bound Good Book and postured himself much like a charismatic Southern Baptist preacher.

"The *Bible* is a library of the songs, poetry, laws, history, mysticism, customs, politics, emotions, wars, humor, hopes and dreams of the Hebrew people. This literature covers thousands of years of evolvement in consciousness of people who believed in one God. Like the individual soul, the souls of a people evolve as their awareness of God is raised. The *Bible* lives through the consciousness of each individual. We each hear from it what we need to hear each time we open it."

He said gently, yet as a matter of fact, "The *Bible* is the textbook for the evolvement of the individual soul. The only thing wrong with it I have ever found is that it has a back cover. It needs no back cover because the *Bible* continues to be written by each of us."

Crash! Ouch! Tough landing. This transporter stuff never hurt on Star Trek. I had departed from a deeply comfortable arrival gate. I had landed in an Oz-like place where the *Bible* and metaphysics were comfortably partnered in the evolvement of human awareness.

I had been metaphysically oriented since childhood (looking beyond the literal of what I read or sensed). I was aware that my life is what I see in it. I knew each mind creates its own world. The human mind will heal, accept and live according to how it thinks. If it is thought to be so, then in the world of that mind it is so. I was of the opinion that the *Bible* took away individual thought through fear and retribution. In my mind, I had unwittingly become prejudiced, closed-minded, and blamed (another word for being a victim) the *Bible*. In my ignorance, I had given power to the traditional teachings with which I disagreed.

Ten minutes earlier. I would have seen such a thought as ludicrous, and labeled the person speaking it ignorant. Surrounded by acceptance, I remembered amber waves of grain and let go. I'd been made aware that I knew nothing about the *Bible*. I wanted to say that wasn't true. I could prove it wasn't true, but I knew that would just be my ego's defense against admitting ignorance. So I let go and I listened.

Don was saying, "Imagine we are part of an ancient Nomadic tribe called the Hebrews. We have traveled all day, and as night falls we gather around the fire. The elders give us stories to answer our most profound questions. What questions would we have in these ancient times?"

We called them out. Don wrote them on his magic board.

"Where do we come from?"

"Why do bad things happen to good people?"

"Why do we have to die?"

"Where do the stars come from?"

"Why are there so many different languages and

colors of people?"

"How come women and men are so different?"

"Why do women give birth and not men?"

"Why are we born naked and then have to wear clothes?"

When our questions filled the board Don began to tell us a story:

"God planted a garden in Eden, and put man there. God also put in Eden every tree that is pleasant to the sight and good for food. He put the tree of life and the tree of the knowledge of good and evil in the garden as well ..."

When he had finished telling his rendition of Adam and Eve, he went to the board and asked which of the questions the story had answered. There was an ionic convergence happening in me. My past intellectual righteousness about the complete idiocy and worthlessness of the *Bible* collided with logic, metaphysics and simplicity. I was hearing a new thought that felt absolutely right-on. When a negative ion meets a positive ion, one will become like the other. I was becoming something new as my mind changed.

Ancient people told stories to teach, to pass on tradition, to educate about the ways of their people. The Hebrews were Nomads. Within these stories the listeners heard what they needed to hear. Maybe in one telling, Eve as the temptress would be blamed for the Fall of Man, Perhaps in another telling, Adam and Eve would simply be the first humans to realize they had individual abilities to discern and have opinions. Still another teller of the tale might focus on the description of the garden to soothe the people tired of the endless sands on which they roamed. No matter the telling, the listeners would be as much a part of the story's meaning as the teller. In this way Nomadic people passed on wisdom, appeased moments of tension, informed without belittling and settled disputes. I understood this concept from my Native American teachings as a child. I got it!

Don spent that week giving us Biblical history, law, and mythology. He never judged our opinion, never made anyone wrong. He simply believed that what you heard, how you judged, and who you blamed was a reflection of where your consciousness was at the time. Your opinion was yours and Don was saying it was none of his business.

I left the Village that week sure that I had been sheep-like for far too many years. I had followed the intellectual herd that was anti-*Bible*. I had taken things literally from a library that was written by a people who were not literal. I had devalued the power of story for the excuse of fact. I had to admit I was a *Bible* bigot. Prejudice is a pet peeve of mine. I believe it is one of humanities most destructive, cruel and self-centered idiocies. To realize I was a bigot shocked me to the core. So I began to do what we do when we are brave enough to admit we are ignorant — I began to educate myself. First I had to let go of things I had adopted from others and willingly seek my own truth.

When I make a decision about another based on what a third party says — I am empowering gossip. I cannot know you through the opinions of others. I need to spend time with you myself. In our time together, I would not want to enter the relationship to prove you are a horrible person. If I did, I would succeed. Instead, my desire is for peace, love, joy and all the good stuff of life, so I would enter a relationship with a mind open to those possibilities. This is how I began my relationship with the *Bible*. No longer would I listen to the *gossip* of a religion, person or society. I would discover for myself what I thought about Scripture. I would discover for myself what I believed.

Retelling Your Story

Knowledge is both the root of separation and the blossom of possibilities. When knowledge is a process it creates new life. When knowledge is an arrival point it creates stagnation and death. One of life's greatest eye opening stories is best summed up with the Shakespearean quote: "Me thinks thou doest protest too much!" In this story *me* is doing the thinking and I am the *thou*. When we argue, resist, prove why a thing cannot be so or a thought cannot be true — it is a sign of desperation. The ego is desperately trying to stay in control, to thwart any change that it has not authorized. My story used to be: "Me thinks thou must protest louder." I have come to realize that when I argue with another it has nothing to do with them, their opinion or point of view. My arguing is not with you, it is with me and my fear.

No person can be convinced of anything against their will. This is one of the great wonders of human creation. So why is it we are so afraid of differences? Do we think we will catch an idea that will overtake our own? Imagine a monochromatic world — how dull would that be? More than dull, it would be impossible to find our Self. We would be unable to distinguish one thing, one person, one thought from another. Diversity is not something to tolerate, it is something to celebrate and protect — it is life itself.

There are things we believe to be absolute truths. We can prove our viewpoint. There are things we want everyone to agree with. I believe that anytime we separate ourselves from others by making them wrong — we are being violent. Let's retell some of these violence-inducing extremes.

1. Think of things you have a strong opinion about and then tell yourself you know nothing. Absolutely nothing! Then tell someone else you know nothing about it, and ask for them to teach you. Notice your reaction when doing this. Acknowledge what happens inside and out.

2. If there is any religion you disagree with, feel is wrong in its beliefs — retell that story. Tell a story about the profound truths of that religion. If you label the religion as violent, learn of the peaceful teachings they hold. Then tell a story from that angle. Also look at the violence in the beliefs you hold. If this is something you refuse to do, take a look at your spiritual or religious beliefs and ask: "Do my beliefs include acceptance and love of

others?" To clarify, acceptance is completely void of ANY judgment.

3.   If you still are not willing then I suggest you get to know people of other beliefs. If you cannot open your hearts to the beauty in all people of all faiths then your story becomes one of judgment, superiority and separation.

Crossed Out

When talking we seek, when silent we find.

~ Teri Hawkins

BACK IN THE LIMOUSINE — THIS TIME ALL ALONE — I waited for the 165 foot, eighty-year-old historic water tower to come into view. When I saw it I knew I was only minutes from my second visit to Unity Village. The village is a 1,500-acre retreat from the highways of traffic that surround it. The 100,000 gallons of fresh water held in the tower are enjoyed by guests, and support some of the most beautiful formal gardens I have witnessed. The architecture has a Mediterranean feel to it and the majority of the land is wilderness. It is home to an abundance of wildlife, including rabbits, deer, a variety of birds and even a cougar now and then. There is a full-size labyrinth, a beautiful outdoor pool, a golf course and an airconditioning system that was an engineering feat for its time. It is a truly prayed-up place — something you feel the minute you breathe its air. I liked this place.

The first time I had been here, my life had been set topsy-turvy by the realization that I was utterly ignorant about something I thought I understood perfectly. I had opened the *Bible* and experienced no burning of flesh or eyes — a surprise, but true none the less. I was still processing this little tidbit, so although I appreciate a good awakening now and then, I was not planning on anything so jarring on this trip. Not that I planned it last time, yet now I was better prepared. I had agreed to take a certain number of classes here at the Village in order to satisfy my obligations to Unity's association. This agreement allowed me to accept a two-year contract as minister to a small church in Coos Bay, Oregon. The first time I'd come, I was completely clueless about what to expect. This time I was much more prepared; I had a plan.

I was going to take two classes on meditation, one on the history of Unity Village, and I was signed up for a hay ride tour of the grounds. I also had a private room this time and planned on a lot of walking, some swimming, healthy food, and of course lots of meditation. I had been practicing meditation for more than twelve years so I felt on steady ground. I was clear that this trip would be void of any life-changing, identity-crashing, ego-slapping revelations. It was a plan. My ego loves plans. My logic loves plans. They like to make plans, follow them, get others on board with them and look back at how well laid they actually were. In reality I believe plans provide some of the best fodder the Universe has for belly laughs.

I settled in that first evening, went to the inn for a uniquely healthy combination of taste treats and then for an enjoyable walk out into the acres of trees, paths and wildlife. I'd brought my putter and found an empty green to practice on while the moon rose orange, the sun set soft and the fireflies came out to dance. The next morning, I awoke to birds singing to the clear blue overhead. I did some yoga stretches, pulled on a cool cotton dress in anticipation of Midwestern humidity, had some fresh strawberries and oatmeal, then off to meditation class.

Much to my chagrin, I tend to be fully human. My humanness comes with a side of habit. One of my consistent habits in life is NOT learning things the first time. I had learned, oh I don't know maybe hundreds of times, that when you make a plan you need to get buy-in from others who are a part of the plan — even if the *others* include the esoteric or outright divine. It seems an obvious basic for success, I know, but one can never underestimate the power of the human ability to deceive itself.

Here I was in the first session, first day, last hour of a meditation class. The teacher asks us to prepare for guided meditation. She provides all the assurances of safety and comfort, and off we fly. Literally, we fly; she is taking us to another place in time. I remember her asking us to look down at our feet and to see sandals upon them, then to look up and ... and ... and after that I have no idea what she said.

What I saw and experienced in that meditation would change a profound story in my life I did not even know I had. It was also a journey that somehow taught me something I'd never heard in my waking hours, yet became an incredible truth in my life.

As the instructor's voice faded from my conscious awareness I was looking down at sandals, and when I looked up there was a walled city before me. I was wearing a kind of cloth wrapped around me like a robe. The fabric was quite soft and equally cool. It was morning, and many people were walking through a large opening that appeared to be a gateway. As I entered the "city" it was nothing but wall-to-wall people. It seemed I knew where I was going. From the surrounding conversations I garnered that something big was happening.

As I followed the flow of the crowd, I was gradually accumulating a tortuous, agonizing sorrow. I knew I was too late. I remember thinking, *What am I late for?*

Then I heard someone in the crowd reporting to a friend, "They nailed him to a cross, and the whole time he was soothing the soldiers, letting them know it was okay."

When I heard these words, I instantly decided to come out of the mediation. I hated anything to do with the whole crucifixion story. For as long as I could remember I disliked crosses. My mother had even bought me one for my high school graduation. I never wore it and got rid of it as fast as I could. I was done with this meditation and I was angry that someone had taken me here. It was time to come out of it. Now! Open your eyes, stand up and walk out of here. Now!

I didn't leave. Instead I found myself leaping on top of an outcropping and looking over the heads of the crowd. There in the distance was a man hanging on a cross. Although the distance between us was great, our eyes met, separated by only a few feet. I knew him. I loved him; we were friends, good friends.

Then I became aware of myself. I was a powerful man, a wealthy man of influence. I spoke from heartbreak and frustration, "Why didn't you send a messenger? Why didn't you let me know? I could have stopped this!"

Then I actually heard his response. To clarify my astonishment, let me try to explain. When I hear something in meditation, it is always inside my head. This was different, I actually heard a whisper in my ear, as one would while in a hug.

He said, "Because I want to be here. This is my destiny; it is for this I came."

My heart broke. It broke like a five-year-old little girl who had just lost her puppy, and with it all the tail wags, face licks and wiggles that soothed her loneliness and supported her happiness. It was a complete, total and pure break. It happened without words — it just shattered.. With the break there was a strange mixture of warmth and a simultaneous sweet and profound gratitude — for what, I had no clue.

I looked into his eyes and he said, "I am not suffering, my beloved friend. Let your heart be at ease, I do not suffer. I am where I want to be and I am not alone. I have thirsted for this experience, this complete acceptance of my being beyond this body."

My sorrow was gone. I felt a pride as a father might feel when he first realizes the greatness in his son. Then I knew I was keeping him from something he deeply desired. That he was here talking to me, not to ask for my help, but to sooth my sorrow. It was not where he really wanted to be. So I let him go. With my heart pouring light from its cracks and crevices, I let him go. I said goodbye. The love in those eyes felt deeply familiar to me, to me, Teri, of the twenty-first century.

I watched myself as I stepped down from the stones I'd been standing upon and began to walk away from the crowd, out of the city. I found a spot to pitch a small tent and I waited. A deep peace came over me and I knew that I had been given a great gift — I just did not know what it was.

Then I opened my eyes, found myself back in class, a towel on my lap, my face itchy from dried tears, and my nose in need of relief. My bodily needs were secondary to the feelings and thoughts demanding my attention. The emotions were deep and true, coming from an unfamiliar place. The thoughts felt like they were mine, but I could not remember ever having had them before.

The eyes of the instructor sitting next to me in silent attention were filled with curiosity about what I'd experienced. I could not talk. I slowly shook my head and she understood. It took a while for me to move. I hugged her and left. I remained silent for the rest of the day. I took walks, drank water, but had no real interest in anything but being inside myself. I felt dichotomies rise and fall within feelings of a gentle caress, deep loss, great honor, high responsibility, calm understanding, and strangest of all, a sense that a dark, empty hole in me that I never knew existed was now filled with light. The instructor had simply asked me to do only what I felt like doing the rest of the day. Being a good student, I did my homework well; I slept, walked, slept, drank water and slept.

The next morning I went to the teacher's office before class. She shared her side of the experience. "You began to sob so deeply that I asked the rest of the class to leave. I sat with you for over an hour. Then you suddenly started breathing very deeply, stopped crying and a deep peacefulness came over you. That entire time you did not move even a fraction."

I reciprocated, sharing as best I could. Graciously she listened and did not question.

When I was finished with my narrative she hugged me, held my shoulders, looked into my eyes and said, "You look like a different person. I think the best thing for you right now is to spend time with who you met yesterday. You might start by going to the mirror and looking in it for a minute ... just to see if you notice anything."

I thanked her and left, going straight to the restroom and a mirror. I saw no difference. My eyes were still blue with hints of laughter in them. My skin color was still freckled with sun-touched pinkness. It was basically the same face the mirror had always offered to me. As I walked out I considered the possibility that I might not be seeing as clearly as I presumed.

Across from the door I was exiting was the other restroom door. Its sign read *Women*. I'd gone into the men's room. Okay, I know that could mean nothing, it could have been just a little quirky coincidence that happens to people who find themselves playing the leading role in an melodramatic farce about their best laid plans. I was actually quit calm about it. Throughout the remainder of the week I easily maintained a deep and clear calmness.

My first day back home, I went for a walk on the beach. I came upon two pieces of driftwood lying in a perfect cross. I reacted out of habit. I rearranged the cross into two parallel lines. My reaction to crosses had been dramatic for as long as I could remember and for the first time I was willing to ask why. Why did I have so much anger about a cross? Where did I get my vehemence about the tales with the cross? This was deeper than just the rationale I had learned. I felt the past week set me up to ask these questions. I could think of no better time than a gentle day on an abandoned beach to seek the answers. I sat in the sand with my back to a dry log of drift wood, looked out to the waves and meditated. This time I was transported back to when I was five years old.

Retelling Your Story

If you have ever been interested in time machines then you will love visioning. Visioning erases the lines between the past, present and future. Visioning is an experience of The Now. This means visioning is a tool of healing, accepting and creating the life we desire.

My process of visioning is not about sitting with work associates and walking through an activity that creates a written declaration of where the company will be in five years that is forgotten in five months. I am also not talking about cutting out pictures from a magazine that represent your dreams. Nor am I referring to affirmations taped to the bathroom mirror to read every morning aloud. I think all of these have value, in fact I have done and enjoyed them all — it just isn't what I am referring to.

To me visioning is an internal human process that creates nothing short of unbelievable miracles. Visioning showed me I would walk again when the "facts" said I would not. Let's open our lives to an everyday use of our own unique visioning power.

1. What flashes of intuition have you had that proved to be right on? Did you listen? When have you not listened? Which do you feel works best for your life? Tell others a story about when your intuition has worked for you. Ask them to share one as well. While you are with that person, share your intuition about him/her when you first met. Ask them to do the same.

2. Have you ever been in a visioning process with others? When you came out of the silence did you have an awareness of a synchronicity between you? Tell yourself that story and tell it to others.

3. Sit in silence and imagine your life as a peaceful, happy, prosperous, free, expansive existence. While imagining go through your senses and use them to *see* the vision. Taste, smell, see, hear, feel what you are imagining. Give yourself at least ten minutes in the visioning, then write about it or tell someone else.

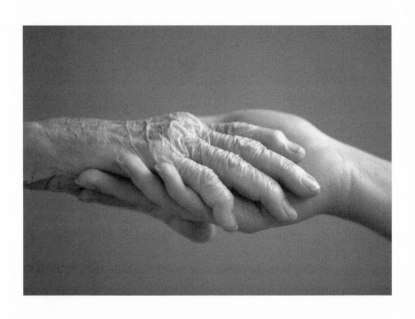

No Goodbye Needed

A child needs a grandparent, anybody's grandparent, to grow a little more securely into an unfamiliar world.

~Charles and Ann Morse

I WAS STYLIN' IN MY 1962 SUNDAY BEST, SPORTING A dark green dress with large white polka dots. The stiff crinoline slip beneath created a bell shape to my narrow five-year-old hips. I was accessorized perfectly with touches of matching green in my white hat, anklets and gloves. The entire little princess ensemble was christened with black patent leather side-buckle shoes and a snappy plastic purse. Inside the purse I had a pink-bordered hankie and a one-dollar bill for the collection basket. My wild red hair was behaving for the moment and it was unusually sunny for a spring day in Oregon. Every thing was perfect.

I climbed into the plastic covered seats of The Hulk, my gramma's giant green Chevy. My legs instantly stuck to the seat but I didn't complain, after all I was a young lady. I sat with my hands in my lap. Once in awhile my purse would call to me to open it. I would comply, retrieve my hankie and dab my nose. It seemed the right thing to do, even if my nose lacked the need. On that special morning, I was the poster child for good behavior and adorability.

Due to the angle at which I looked out of The Hulk's windshield, my view of our journey was primarily of evergreen tops in a backdrop of blue. When the steeple of our destination finally came into view, a swarm of Monarchs made their home in my tummy. This was the day, the big day. I was going to *big-people* church with my grandmother. I felt so grown-up and sincerely wanted to make Gramma proud. I had attended Sunday School at her Catholic church several times, but I had never been through the fronts door of the big-people's church. Today that was all going to change. It felt like a rite of passage from babyhood to young girl.

Without warning or permission, a wild red curl bounded out from beneath my hat. I could not get it to go back, lie down, or straighten out. My mother lived by the theory that my wild, unmanageable hair was a perfect reflection of my personality. On this day I was clearly proving my mother wrong. My grandmother's faith in me was winning the day. I could be a good girl. I knew I could. My hair was not boss over me, and moms can be wrong — really they can. As we came up to the grand doors of the chapel, the priest bent down to welcome me. I curtsied adorably, then obediently stood silently clutching my handbag as Gramma and the Father carried on a torturously long conversation.

My intense desire to go to big-people church had begun at about age three. It was the first time since I was an infant that I was to spend the night with my maternal grandmother with whom I felt a singular bond. My mother had two explanations for this special affection. One perfectly logical: "I was so sick when you were born that she kept you the first six weeks of your life". The other, perfectly Mom: "You're just like her."

To me Gramma was this energetic, strong woman who laughed a lot and thought I was a great kid. She made me feel special even though she had umpteen grandchildren. She baked the best oatmeal chocolate chip cookies in the universe and sewed the latest fashions for my one and only doll. I genuinely adored Gramma Madge, and in so doing, found my first unique family role as the one who didn't fear her.

Soon after Mom and I arrived for my stay-over with Gramma, I noticed a picture on the wall in the living room. It was of a man with long brown hair. He was beautiful. All around him were happy, cute, little children and lambs. Standing behind several other tots was a little red-haired girl. I took the picture down and climbed up on Gramma's lap.

"This little girl looks just like me."

Gramma looked and said, "It sure does — look at that beautiful hair."

That was Gramma! My hair was beautiful to her.

I looked hopefully into her eyes and asked, "Is this my father?"

"You know that isn't your father, sister. That's Jesus."

"Who is Jesus?"

At this, my grandmother became serious, turning severe eyes upon my mother. "This child does not know who Jesus is?"

The conversation became too grown-up and boring for me. I took my picture of Jesus and we went up to the hayloft to play. I learned a lot about Jesus that day. I learned that Jesus liked little girls with wild red hair; that he was gentle, safe and protective. I found out he was kind of silly and we laughed big time when my dog started snoring. I found out that he didn't like arguing anymore than I did. We tossed rocks at fence posts below and would cheer when we hit one. If you ever have the chance to see Jesus do a victory dance — take it. I lacked a strong father figure in my life, and Jesus seemed perfect for the role. We talked a lot, I even felt him hug me one time — just because. I had made a special friend: it was a sweet day, one I wanted to remember forever.

At the age of three, I fought going to bed. I always thought I might miss something. Warm milk would leave me wanting cocoa. Bedtime stories hurled me into my own version of the ending. Playing hard until I dropped left everyone else exhausted and me ready for more. Yet, after spending that afternoon in the hayloft with my new friend, all I needed was his picture beside my bed. I went straight to sleep. From then on, bed time at Gramma's was easy as long as I had the picture with me. Jesus and I had a lot to talk about. I told him things I couldn't tell anyone, and he shared his heart with me as well. There were times he asked my opinion with genuine interest in my response. He and I were special buddies.

Jesus was with me that Saturday night before I was to go to the big-people's church. He sat framed beside my bed and yet was free in my thoughts. Both of us knew we had been friends before I was ever born. It was something we got about each other. He had such a great sense of humor. I think he is the one who first taught me to laugh at myself. He never spanked me and he always, always made me feel safe. He was so tender and he loved me, and I loved him as only a little child loves. I remember that now — how much I loved him.

Gramma told me I would learn more about Jesus when I was a little older. I wasn't sure there was anyone who could tell me something about him I didn't already know. Yet, I did love going to Gramma's church and listening to the Sisters retell stories Jesus once told long ago. A parable that profoundly touched me was the one with all the seeds. I had been called a bad seed several times already in my short years. Jesus and I were such good friends that I knew this story was telling me that there are no bad seeds, only better places to plant them if you want them to grow up to be beautiful and healthy. I was going to plant myself someplace good. I thought I would need his help and decided I wanted to have a big-person friendship with him. The next step for me was obviously to go to big-people church. For months, I pestered Mom and Gramma. Mom was against it — she didn't think I could hold still that long, and Gramma had a serious conversation with me about how I was to behave. I made a lot of promises and won the right to go.

My demure wait upon the steps was over, the epic conversation between Gramma and the Father, complete. We faced the grand double doors and walked through. Gramma dipped her fingers in an angelically supported stone water basin and made the sign of the cross. I echoed the process, displaying to all that I belonged there. We began to walk down the aisle. Sunlight danced through a huge multi-colored window high up on one wall. I must have forgotten to breathe and hiccuped loudly, receiving my first "Shhhh" of the morning. I grabbed Gramma's hand, looked up into the arched roof, and then turned to see the huge pipes standing in attention behind a bunch of people dressed in dark navy blue robes. This was better than even my imagination had produced. When I turned back, the grownup legs that had previously blocked my view of the altar were gone. I froze. Something was terribly wrong. The butterflies in my gut flew away to be replaced by an ice cube of terror. There before me, without warning, was a man hanging from a huge cross. He was almost naked and had nails in his hands and feet. The scene was gruesome, yet what gripped me was a feeling that I knew who it was.

I tugged on Gramma asking quietly, "Gramma, who is that?"

She looked up and flatly declared, "Sister, don't be

silly. That's your Jesus."

I looked at her, and I looked at the horror before me. I wanted to scream, *It is not!* I also wanted to keep my promises to Gramma and prove her trust in me. So I tried what little I knew of being more mature: "Why is he up there?" Then I added a sincere statement of fact: "We have to help him."

Gramma grabbed me severely and whisper-yelled, "Young lady, you will sit down and be the good girl you promised me you'd be."

I sniffled, pinched my lips together and tried, I really tried. Then I glanced up, saw my friend and burst into tears: "We have to help him, Gramma. He would help me. I have to get him down. Please help me."

I was ready to climb up on that platform and help him down. I knew I could do it. I knew I could, and I knew he would do it for me. I also knew with Gramma on my side, I would be unstoppable.

Gramma grabbed my arm and sat me down. My wild red-haired consciousness took over. From the roots of my being, I just could not sit down or straighten out. I had to break loose. I squirmed free and went running in tears and screams down the aisle.

"Get him down, somebody has to help me get him down."

I was overcome with terror and grief. I felt a deep core of helplessness and loneliness building in me. It is my earliest memory of devastation. I was swept up in folds of black fabric, swung over an ample shoulder, and swatted firmly on the behind. I jumped and went stiff and still. My rump was familiar with swats and spankings, so it was not from physical pain I froze — it was the look on the face of my grandmother following behind. I had broken my promises to her. She was ashamed of me. I was an embarrassment. I wept from a place no five-year old should ever know. I had betrayed my grandmother's trust, let down a dear friend, and all for nothing.

It was a Sister of the church who had halted my rescue attempt. My grandmother accompanied us as I was taken to a little, gray room. They tried to console me by making me understand that what I had done was wrong. They told me that Jesus died for my sins. They were basically telling me I was responsible for him being up there on that cross. I knew that was not true. There was nothing about him that was suffering or judgmental, and he certainly was not dead. I also knew that he would never think I was some kind of sinner — he thought I was fun and kind and good. In that moment I realized that as wrong as I believed them to be, they were not going to listen to me. To both women I was a five-year-old girl who knew nothing about Jesus.

But I did know. I knew to the core of my being that Jesus was still alive. I knew that if I persisted in that knowing, I would lose my gramma. I knew I had a choice to make, Gramma or Jesus. I knew a lot, but not enough to figure out how to keep both my friend and my grandmother. I lost so much that day. I remember that now — how lost I was. When we got home, I took the picture from beside my bed and placed it back on the wall. I never again slept with that picture and avoided it at all costs. I became painfully aware of the crosses around Gramma's house and what they meant. Her heart and home remained a warm retreat for the rest of my life. My conversations with Jesus, however, stopped. I didn't even say goodbye.

Retelling Your Story

The happiest, most free, silliest, most curious, accepting, wise and loving creatures I know are children — especially the ones not yet tainted by adult claims of right and wrong. When little kids get in a fight they get mad and get over it. If adults will stay out of it the kids will be back playing together in minutes.

The Declaration of Independence states that everyone has the right to pursue happiness. I never did get that. When I was eleven, I remember thinking, *If I pursue it, won't that make it run away?* Children don't pursue happiness, they live it, breath it, find it wherever they can in the moment. A child is happy making an empty toilet paper roll into a horn. A child is happy just looking at Mom and Dad holding hands on the couch watching TV. A child is happy watching the trees zoom by from the car window.

Let's start with you and me in rewriting the hierarchy of our world. Let's put kids at the top. Let's start saying to ourselves, "What would children do?" Let's honor the simplicity of a child as we honor that of the great mystics and luminaries of the world. Here are some ideas:

1. Identify a concern in your life and then ask a child what they think you should do. Really listen for the wisdom.

2. Ask a child to teach you how to be happier. What do they think you need to do more of? Less of? Then try it.

3. Ask a child if they would rather live in a big house and play with Mom or Dad once in a while, or live in a little house and play with Mom or Dad every day?

4. Tell a child at every opportunity how amazing they are, and ask forgiveness every time you say anything that implies otherwise.

5. Think back on the things you use to do for fun when you were a child. Then go do your favorites with the friends you have now.

6. Tell a story of how your adult life differs from your childhood. Think of how you react, feel, think and want differently than you used to do.

7. Play with kids at least once a week. If you are a parent, at least three times a week.

8. Ask a child what they would do to change the way the world is today.

C.B., Me Tig and the Angel

I have been on the verge of being an angel all my life, but it hasn't happened yet.

~ Mark Twain

It was time for bed. First I would gather up my courage, run to the window, close my eyes and shut the curtains. I did not want to see if the homicidal maniac was outside my window or not. All I knew was that once the curtains were closed, I was safe on that front. Then I would push my bed away from the wall. Lifting up the covers quickly, I would make sure there were no bedbugs in my bed. Once satisfied, I would tuck all corners of the sheets, blankets and bedspread into the mattress and place a carnivorous stuffed animal at each one of the four legs — this was of course to prevent any snakes, spiders, rats or mice from getting to me in the night.

Me Tig (a tiger) would be placed facing the closet — he was the best at keeping monsters away. I don't know what it was that made Me Tig so good at this — I guessed it was his laughter. He laughed a lot, truly a silly tiger. Once he took over closet patrol, all the monsters moved out. Then came Cinnamon Bear, my oldest and bestest friend. He was the constant in my childhood. He had moved with me to every new bedroom I had ever had. No matter the new creatures that may be lurking to attack — with C.B. I was safe. Of that I never doubted. I was given C.B. on the day I was born. My dad had brought him to the hospital. Fifty years later, he sits upon a rocker in my bedroom and wouldn't want to be anywhere else. He is older now, but I would still match him up against the most vicious of imaginary creatures

— no contest! C.B.'s station was atop my headboard. The rest of the stuffed animals would be put under the window just in case the curtains leaked darkness. Then I would get dressed for bed, brush my teeth, tell Mom good night and return to my room. I would grab Cotton Candy (a pink and white bear) and put my hand on the light switch. I would check with C.B., get thumbs-up, take a deep breath, and with perfect timing, switch off the light and dive for my bed simultaneously.

Even with all the safeguards, there were nights when I was scared out of my wits. I know people think you can't see in the dark — but I could, and I didn't like what I saw.

On these nights something else happened — something more calming than my mother's voice and more real than all the stuffed animals in existence. At the height of terror, I would hear a chair rocking and someone softly humming. Instantly, the terror would be gone. I would open my eyes and there, in the corner of my room, sat a gentle old man, looking right at me, smiling and humming. Sometimes he would be singing a song; it was a song my mom often sang: "K-K-K-Katie, beautiful Katie…." His voice was kind of rusty but it was simple and soothing. He was balding and not very tall, a slight man with a kindness that I never questioned. I would stare into his eyes — which, by the way, were mirrors of love.

He would always say the same thing, "I'm here now, my girl; nothin' can harm you. I'm always here, just thought you needed remindin'."

Then he would smile, rock slowly, and I would usually fall right to sleep. That was it.

We shared a few short conversations over the years, usually right after we moved to a new house. It took few words for him to convince me that I would be alright, that he would always be there, and that he loved me. I never doubted him. In all my wild imaginings — which you can probably deduce were plentiful — I never feared that man, and I began to call him my angel. Of course I didn't tell anyone, and my stuffed animals were sworn to secrecy.

When I was in my late thirties, it became time for my maternal gramma to move to an assisted care facility. I drove down to help pack things up. While cleaning out her dresser, I came across an antique nylon stocking crammed at the back of a little side drawer. Inside were old pictures. As I thumbed through them I froze. It is one of those moments where life as we know it changes and we are unsure of our next move. I was holding a picture of my angel. I walked into the living room and asked my grandmother who it was in the picture. She told me it was Earle Craine, her second husband who had been killed in a logging accident.

It was September 20th, 1957. Earle was on his way

to work when he thought he would stop by the hospital to see my mother; she was going to have a baby... me! The pregnancy was difficult and she had been in the hospital for a few days. Earle loved my mother as if she were his own daughter. He'd stopped just to give her a hug and put his vote in for a girl.

He told her, "Kaye, you have my girl for me now."

Every story I ever heard of this man was filled with warmth, comfort and kindness. I grew up loving him very much. Since the first time I'd met my angel, I always wanted it to be Grampa Craine — so I pretended it was.

I had never told anyone about my angel, not even my gramma who with her devout Catholicism was big on angels. I was just never sure if her idea of angels included a sweet old man in work boots and a rocking chair sitting in the corner of my room at night. That day when she told me that my angel was my Grampa Craine, I was so astonished, so knocked off my sense of reality that I just blurted it out.

Her response was perfect. She looked at me and said, "I am not surprised. He loved you very much. He was so excited to have a granddaughter. I'm glad you got to meet him. He was a kind, loving man."

Gramma reached for the stocking I'd taken from the deep recesses of her dresser and dug inside. She pulled out a box with a ring in it. It was her wedding ring from Earle.

She placed it in my hand, curled my fingers around it and said: "It's yours sweetheart; now your angel will be with you wherever you go."

As I look at it on my little finger, writing this story, tears fill my eyes — he's here. I don't see him physically anymore; I haven't since the day I got the ring. I guess he knows now I will never forget him and that he is always near.

As I read this story to my mom over the phone, she stops me with a sharp intake of breath. I asked, "What's wrong, Mom?"

She answers by singing, "K-K-K-Katie, beautiful Katie. You're the only G-G-G-Girl that I adore….."

Tears interrupt the song and she whispers in a warm awe, "Sis, Earle always sang that song to me, he was singing it as he walked out of my room at the hospital the day he died. Twelve hours later, you were born and I never saw him again."

We were both silent for a bit. There is nothing more to do in a moment like this than to share it in silence.

Finally I said, "He loved you, Mom".

"I know he did, Sis."

I continued: "I think he wanted you to know that you would always be okay too. I'm sorry I never delivered the message."

I guess if I had, both our lives would have been a different story.

Retelling Your Story

There will never be a day when we have all the answers, never a time when we will be able to do it all on our own, never a moment without angels all around us. There are countless happenings in life that open our eyes to the impossible, the magical, the miraculous and awe-inspiring. We just have to stop and listen to the messengers of the moment. These angels come clothed as a moment shared with a stranger, ease offered by an animal, answers in a song's lyrics or awareness found in a falling leaf. They may have wings, they may not. Someone else may believe what you experience, others may not. It is up to you whether you want to have mystery in the story of your life. Just because something cannot be proved or explained does not mean it isn't true. If it offers you peace and joy, I say, "Go for it!"

I. Have you ever had an experience that was beyond what you label as *reality* (a miracle, an intuition, a vision, a dream, etc.)? List them, then tell the story to someone as a matter of fact, not as just a possibility. Then ask them to share a magical story with you. This is a much better way to create a great friendship than sharing how we slept last night or how our parents are driving us nuts.

2. Write down the names of three people who have been *angels* in your life.

3. Now write down the names of three people with whom you've had your greatest challenges. Include public figures, strangers or loved ones. Retell your story about them, making them the greatest angels in your life.

4. How has this book been a messenger for you? What wisdoms have you heard in the identifying and telling of stories along the way? I know you have been an angel to me, I just am not sure how — I may never know how, but I know it is so. So, thank you.

THERE IS ALWAYS A HAPPILY EVER AFTER AVAILABLE, yet never is there an end to the story of your life. You are without question a magnificent tale waiting to be heard. It is my desire that you have, in even a small way, realized that your life is the story you make it. May it be a tale that inspires, uplifts and heals the world around you. Thank you for the time you have given to the words I have offered. I appreciate your trust and I honor your story.

Blessings, Teri

4 Free Gifts
Valued at $75.00
Teri just wants to thank you for reading
Life Retold. Go to:
www.liferetold.com/gifts

If you loved the book enough to recommend it to a friend or give it as a gift that would be so wonderful, however the gifts are yours regardless.

Your Gifts of thanks include:

Teri Hawkins Live! Teri is a world class speaker and this downloadable CD has 8 short, inspirational, spiritually centered talks that range from 7 to 14 minutes in length. The perfect support to start a great day or get out of a cloudy one. Value: $20.00

New Space. A magnificent quantum poetry book, (downloadable) by Sam Smith. (The poems found at the front and back of Life Retold are his). Many people who are neutral about poetry are fascinated by this poet. Value: $20.00

Godsong. A downloadable CD of award winning sing along songs in the spiritual genre. Even non-singers will appreciate the healing medicine of these simplistic supportive tunes. Value: $20.00

Mythology Guided Inner Journeys. A downloadable CD of 3 mediations to assist you subconsciously with the retelling of your stories. By Jane Meyers. Value: $15.00

All yours free at:
www.liferetold.com/gifts
Thank you, Teri

Also by Teri Hawkins:

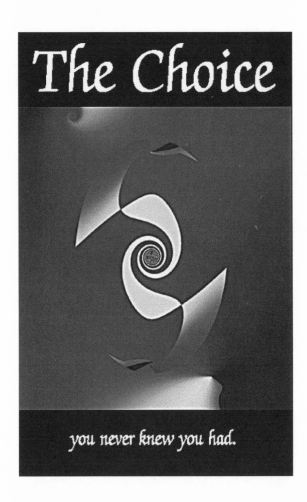

The Choice

you never knew you had.

The Choice is a thoroughly unique experience that begins by honoring your own innate wisdom. It then weaves an eclectic offering of heart-captivating stories, thought-provoking activities, brain-tickling poetry, energy-releasing music, life-supporting synergy and soul-illuminating inner journeys. These elements all combine to draw knowledge from your head, transforming it through your heart, into wisdom for your life.

For more information go to:
www.4thechoice.com

Services by Teri:

World Class Coach

Teri learned how to be a champion from championship coaches. This is how she coaches – to your greatness, through your wisdom, toward your dreams.

For more information go to:
www.liferetold.com

Keynote Speaker

Og Mandino, after hearing Teri talk the first time, said, "You touched his heart, her intellect and my soul – you honored, challenged and accepted everyone here. Thank you."

For more information go to:
www.liferetold.com

Retreats

Laughter, music, silence, connection, healing, awakening — all happen at Teri's eclectic offering of retreats. As a shaman of the animal lore, Unity minister, student of ancient Aramaic, a vocalist, lyricist and songwriter, Teri deeply enjoys leading retreats.

For more information go to:
www.liferetold.com

Seminars

Teri never does the same seminar twice — REALLY! She is what is known as a Socratic teacher. This means she believes the only answers worth finding are those that come from within the wisdom of the individual.

For more information go to:
www.liferetold.com

Ants and Elephants

The source of your life
is the source of my life —
an ant arises from the
same energy as an elephant —
a tube worm clinging to its
undersea vent
is as close to God
as the Dalai Lama —
a baby crying in Beijing
uses lungs as marvelous
as the child screaming in delight
at Disneyland —
your life is my life —
no heart beats
no synapse fires
that is not the consciousness
of God —
God has countless eyes
and countless tongues —
but one heart...
when we cut ourselves from this
with the knives of
hate and envy and
revenge,

with the illusions
of lies and war
and separation
the blackness that swallows us
is an isolation of our own design —
we are not separate...
the source of your life
is the source of my life —
my breath is your breath
your blood is my blood
your love is my love —
we are together the Universe
gasping wide-eyed
into consciousness —
one slippery expressive being —
your hands are my hands
my words are your words —
we are not separate
my life
your life
one Source

~ Sam Smith

Rest

To climb the mountain of
enlightenment —
rest.
Lay down the sharpened axe
of effort —
put aside the ropes of
striving
and stop.

Awakening waits
to cradle you
wherever you lay
your head —
angels shine and
stars sing
when you rest
in the soft place prepared
for you —
the soft place that is
everywhere…

You will not see
the face of God by
standing on a stack
of books —
to hear the song of stars
and to see the light of angels
close your eyes —
rest your head
and open your heart to
the soft
safe place
you are

~ Sam Smith

The Story of Your Tasting

The stars in the sky
tell their story
of mythic beasts
and maidens fair —
of snakes
and dogs
and hunters —
and yet the stars are balls of
hydrogen fusion
unimaginable to the mind
making up this story —
the mind that sees the constellations
and sifts through
the facets of
a fractured day...
making sense of the clues —
knitting up the plot.

The story of this moment lies
in your eyes
and in your fingertips
touching lightly
every surface
and in your lungs as
you breathe
and in your tongue as
you taste
and speak —
telling the story of your tasting —
in every inspiration and in
every expiration —
the story of your tasting...

Every atom is the tongue of God
tasting its creation —
every star knows
the fragrance of the Universe —
a scent
a sense
a feeling —
the story
of
you.

                              ~ Sam Smith

Angel

The sweet voice of your good news
May be difficult to hear
When that voice is
A color
When those words are
A ripple
When that guidance is
a misty morning
A flock of sparrows
A glance
A touché
A whisper
In the drumbeat of
Your heart
It may be difficult to hear
But listen

That whisper is
An invitation
To your joy-
A joy as loud as
Trumpets

~ Sam Smith